Aston Martin and Lagonda
Volume 2: V8 models from 1970

Aston Martin and Lagonda

Volume 2: V8 models from 1970

A collector's guide
by Paul Chudecki

MOTOR RACING PUBLICATIONS LTD
Unit 6, The Pilton Estate, 46 Pitlake, Croydon CR0 3RY, England

First Published 1990

British Library Cataloguing in Publication Data

Chudecki, Paul
   Aston Martin and Lagonda.
   Vol. 2 ; V8 models from 1970
   1. Aston Martin and Lagonda cars
   I. Title
   629.2222

ISBN 0-947981-41-1

Typeset in Great Britain by
Ryburn Typesetting Ltd, Halifax, West Yorkshire

Printed in Great Britain by
The Amadeus Press Ltd, Huddersfield, West Yorkshire

Contents

Introduction and acknowledgements

As a motoring journalist I cover a great variety of cars, from the mundane to the exotic, but amongst them all Aston Martin has always represented a very special marque. Its sheer pedigree, its wealth of racing experience, the build quality of the hand-crafted British supercars it produces and, not least, their considerable charisma mark them apart, amongst the all-time motoring greats. It is no coincidence that I belong to the Aston Martin Owners Club and I was delighted to agree to write this second Aston Martin and Lagonda book in the Collector's Guide series, though at the same time saddened, the opportunity to do so having come about after the untimely death of Andrew Whyte. Andrew had already written the first volume on Aston and Lagonda six-cylinder cars – a must for any enthusiast of the two marques – and he had been scheduled to write this second accompanying volume when fate intervened.

Throughout this book it will be seen that the DBS V8 is referred to as a Series 1 model and thereafter the AM V8s from Series 2 to 5. Similar designations are used for Lagonda models, but it should be stressed that these designations are not those of the factory, but rather of the AMOC, and have been devised to simplify identification between models when significant changes were introduced. The system has long been used by the AMOC and is now accepted by enthusiasts and car traders alike. I have also included chapters on the use of the Aston V8 engine in competition, and although this has not always been in an Aston Martin-built car, the lessons learnt have invariably been passed on to the production models. It is sad to note, however, that the Aston racing flag will now only be flown by enthusiastic amateurs in club events, politics having killed off the factory's promising 1989 return to international sports car racing.

Compiling a book such as this requires both research and the inevitable assistance of individuals and organizations in confirming facts and records, selecting photographs, etcetera, and in particular I must thank the Aston Martin Owners Club, whose archives and well-maintained Register made my task immeasurably easier, and my special thanks must go to Brian Joscelyne for his assistance with additional photographic material. Valuable assistance was also provided by Aston Martin Lagonda, Richard Williams, Robin Hamilton, Roger Stowers and Richard Zethrin, while a special 'Thank you' is due to Roger Kohn and John Cope for kindly providing their Astons (V8 Series 4 and DBS V8, respectively) for the front cover photograph, which was taken on Newport Pagnell's outskirts. The unregistered Virage (chassis number 3) was briefly pinched off the end of the 'production line'!

Any Aston Martin or Lagonda, by definition, is automatically a collector's car – witness the ludicrous prices paid for early Virages to avoid the waiting list, or the king's ransom needed to acquire a limited-edition V8 Vantage or Volante Zagato, let alone a DB4 GT Zagato. During 1989 in particular auction house prices rose dramatically as non-motoring speculators and other 'investors' entered and distorted the market. However, some of them seem to have caught a cold and as others have run for cover 'hammer prices' have since eased somewhat and by the spring of 1990 had assumed once again a modicum of sensibility. One can only hope that they will continue to do so and that at least some Aston Martins and Lagondas will continue to be within the reach of the true enthusiast and collector. All the models described in this book offer their own particular blend of enjoyable, luxurious and exciting motoring so, if you do buy one as a result, don't just cosset it – drive it, and have fun!

Paul Chudecki
April 1990

This painting, by John Evans, was commissioned by Victor Gauntlett to depict four contemporary AML models, the Vantage, Volante, Lagonda and Bulldog.

Designer Tadek Marek, partly hidden behind one of the four Weber twin-choke carburettors, stands modestly alongside one of his early 5-litre Aston Martin V8 engines. As with its six-cylinder predecessor, much of the engine's early development would take place on the race track.

CHAPTER 1

V8 development

Marek's masterpiece

As a car manufacturer, Aston Martin has endured and survived many crises since the marque was founded in 1914, even facing extinction in the hands of some of its several owners. Of the latter, David Brown, who merged the company with Lagonda, was responsible for putting Aston Martin firmly back on the road to success in the postwar era and it is through the V8 engine, produced in the later years of his tenure, that this success has been able to continue, albeit with a few hiccups, into the 1990s. Now, of course, that V8, which ran for the first time 25 years ago, has been given a new four-valve-per-cylinder lease of life in the Virage. It should guarantee the Aston V8's position as the main powerplant for the exclusive roadgoing products of Newport Pagnell well into the 21st century.

This fact, no doubt, would have pleased the late Tadek Marek, the designer of the original V8 back in the early 'sixties. It was he who was given the brief to draw up a suitable replacement for the Aston six-cylinder, an engine which he had also designed, which in various forms had powered the DB4, DB5, DB6 and DBS Aston Martins. After the V12 designed by colleague Professor Robert Eberan von Eberhorst in the early 'fifties had proved too complex and unreliable for production without financially prohibitive modifications, and at a time when David Brown, John Wyer and others at Aston Martin felt anyhow that the V12 configuration would generally give way to the V8, it was dropped. Eberhorst, who had joined Aston Martin from ERA, having previously been with Auto Union, soon left the company, his position as chief engineer then being taken by Marek.

Plans to produce a V8 thus date back to the late 'fifties, though it was not until 1963 that Marek actually set to work on the new engine. By now the robust alloy six had been stretched in production form to 3,995cc for the DB5 while a 4,164cc version produced as a prototype was shelved when tests highlighted excessive weaknesses between the cylinder bores and around the main bearing caps – although various competition outings with the 4,164cc engine fitted to two DBR2s produced several first and second places in the USA. Of these, Stirling Moss' entry in the 1959 Nassau Trophy race, in which his DBR2 retired, marked the last works race entry of an open Aston Martin; the private entry of George Constantine went on to win.

Even if stretched versions of the 4-litre six had proved reliable they would only have been a stopgap measure, David Brown from an early stage having been keen for Aston to have a low-stressed high-performance engine that could be used for production models well into the company's future – this had been the idea behind the initial development of Eberhorst's Lagonda-intended V12. The capacity of the new V8 was determined by this consideration and by Brown's desire to produce in the 'sixties a faster grand tourer than ever before that could carry four people in comfort and match the acceleration and top speed of Europe's finest.

To this end Marek used the DB5 as his baseline and by determining the required increase in weight and frontal area, combined with the additional power needed to provide the extra performance, he calculated that the new V8 must produce 32% more power than that of the 3,995cc six, which suggested a capacity of around 5.3 litres for between 300 and 350bhp. To begin with, however, engine sizes of 4.6 to 5.4 litres were considered and the first prototype had a capacity of 4,806cc, which was achieved by using a stroke of 83mm with the 96mm bore of the 4-litre six. The latter's use was quite deliberate, the known reliability and power of the six-cylinder engine having led to the decision to incorporate as much of its componentry and design as practically possible into the new V8, which would be given an alloy block and heads. The pistons, bearing patterns, profiles for the twin overhead camshafts per bank, the valves and valve gear (together with 11 sprockets) from the six were thus all incorporated, although to reduce width the valve angle was changed to 64 from 80 degrees.

The first new V8 engine, code-numbered DP 218, was completed on July 29, 1965 and bench-testing began on the same day. Running with four downdraught twin-choke Weber 46 IDA carburettors and with a compression ratio of 8.36:1, initial power was recorded as 275bhp at 5,750rpm. After minor induction tuning this was raised to 285bhp at 6,000rpm and 275lb/ft of torque was recorded at 4,500rpm, the latter figures an improvement on those for the 3,995cc six-cylinder Vantage engine. Although the Vantage was officially quoted as producing 325bhp, it should be remembered that this figure was considerably inflated by Aston in an effort to show parity with vastly exaggerated American bhp figures; the 4-litre Vantage engine's true power output was about 280bhp. Power of the V8 was again increased with the help of compression ratio and induction changes, reaching a peak of 329bhp at 6,200rpm (an AE-Brico fuel injection-equipped engine had produced 325bhp) after more than 100 hours of testing, though some main bearing oil starvation was evident, due in part to crankshaft plugs working loose. In this state of tune, the V8 was fitted to a DB5, the performance of which was somewhat enhanced with a genuine 329bhp on tap!

In the meantime, World Champion motorcyclist turned racing car driver John Surtees had approached Aston Martin with regard to using a much-modified V8 engine for the 1967 World Sportscar Championship. The company, with its considerable racing pedigree, immediately warmed to the idea, though Tadek Marek was very much against his new design being used for competition applications. Nonetheless, an iron-block Chevrolet 5.9-litre V8 engine, similar to that fitted to the Lola T70 campaigned by Surtees in 1966 – and with which he went on to win the World Sportscar Championship – was delivered to Newport Pagnell for evaluation. Using the 412bhp American engine as a baseline, Aston's engineers changed their V8 engine's bore to 97.5mm, but retained the same 83mm stroke, thus increasing the capacity to 4,983cc. The capacity increase, together with a 9.1:1 compression ratio and quadruple Weber 45 DCOE sidedraught carburettors, pushed power up to 332bhp at 5,500rpm and in this tune the Aston V8 was road-tested in a converted DB4. Development continued, with further modifications such as high-lift camshafts and a carburettor change back to 48 IDA downdraught Webers resulting in an impressive 421bhp at 6,500rpm and 386lb/ft of torque at 5,000rpm, the latter figure comparing most favourably with the larger and heavier Chevrolet's 398lb/ft at 4,500rpm.

CHAPTER 2

Racing refines the V8

The Lola-Aston Martins

Originally it had been planned to run one of the company's project race cars, DP 215, with the first V8 engine, but Aston Martin's withdrawal from competitions in 1963 precluded this. However, that year Eric Broadley had designed and launched his 4.2-litre Ford V8-powered Lola GT, the first of a series of successful mid-engined competition cars, the latest of which by the end of 1966 was the Lola T70 MkIII, a derivative of the car which had been used that season by Surtees.

There was also an open version of the Lola known simply as the MkIII, and the Aston V8, now with a capacity of 5,064cc following a cylinder bore increase of 0.5mm to 98mm, was fitted into one of these for shakedown tests, David Hobbs being engaged to carry out the driving. A big-end failure and resultant sheared connecting rod led to the fitment of stronger bearing caps, dry-sump lubrication being adopted at the same time. Further track tests, however, resulted in another con-rod breakage and inspection revealed the oilways to be over-stressed, necessitating their repositioning and strengthening. At the same time, cylinder head modifications and the adoption of higher-lift exhaust camshafts raised peak power to 450bhp at 6,000rpm, torque also being increased to 413lb/ft at 5,000rpm. Both figures easily surpassed those of the 5.9-litre Chevrolet V8 and Aston's engineers were confident they had a fully competitive engine.

The Lola T70 MkIII was launched at the 1967 Racing Car Show at Olympia, where it was announced that although customer cars would be powered by a 460bhp Chevrolet engine, the two Lola factory entries for the season would be equipped with Aston Martin's all-new 5-litre V8 motor. This was the first opportunity for the motoring public to glimpse the new Aston engine, and those who attended the Racing Car Show could inspect the V8 displayed out of the car on the Surtees Racing stand. It was notable, however, that Tadek Marek had sustained his resistance to his new V8 being used for competition and that it was John Wyer who had encouraged David Brown to have racing specification engines built and supplied to Lola Cars. Although Aston Martin at the time still refused to disclose brake horsepower figures (an alternative solution to matching exaggerated American figures) it was suggested that the 5,064cc V8 was probably producing 450bhp, which many felt would be sufficient to provide the Lola-Aston Martin with a very competitive performance.

The first Aston-engined car, bearing the chassis number SL73/101 and now officially known as a Type 73, made its debut at the Nürburgring 1,000kms race, fitted with Lucas fuel injection which, although it reduced power by 13bhp, was felt would alleviate difficulties experienced in pre-Le Mans testing in revving beyond 6,100rpm. Concurrent with those tests had been evidence of cracking around the main bearing housing in the less powerful production-tune engines, and Dural rather than steel caps were fitted to counteract differential expansion, a modification also incorporated into the race engines, although these had not shown similar symptoms. Encouragingly, Surtees recorded the second fastest time in practice at the Nürburgring against opposition from Porsche, Alfa-Romeo, Ferrari, Chaparral and John Wyer's J W Automotive Gulf Mirages.

The Aston Martin V8 engine in one of the Lola-Aston Martins. Although still bearing the original 5-litre version's cam covers. the engine in SL73/101, the first of the two Lola-Astons, is now a 5,340cc unit.

Unfortunately, a rear suspension wishbone broke on the seventh lap of the race and the Lola-Aston's early retirement dented somewhat the team's hopes for a good result from the planned two-car entry at Le Mans.

The second Lola-Aston, bearing the chassis number SL73/121, had by now been built and including the fuel-injected engine used at Nürburgring there were now three race-specification engines. In preparation for the French classic some wind-tunnel tests were conducted at the Motor Industry Research Association (MIRA) to determine the car's optimum drag coefficient, and alterations to ride height, spoilers and the underbody tray improved the drag figure from 0.453 to an eventual Le Mans specification of 0.376, a figure that Marek had calculated would give the Lola a top

speed of 206mph along Le Mans' infamous Mulsanne Straight. However, the continuing reluctance of the Aston V8 to rev was thought to be exacerbated by turbulence around the engine's air intake and to counteract this the newer car, SL73/121, sported revised and longer rear bodywork formed in alloy, which also reduced weight by 59lb compared to the sister car, SL73/101. It was also decided to run both cars with fuel injection, the newer car to be driven by Surtees and Hobbs and the Nürburgring machine by Chris Irwin and Peter de Klerk.

At Le Mans, however, both cars soon developed minor overheating problems in practice and the need to renew the head gaskets, believed to be the cause, prevented the Lola-Astons from completing the session. Cooper seal rings were

An attractive shot of the Lola-Aston which amply shows off the sports-car's beautiful lines.

The same car, SL73/101, at speed at an AMOC Brands Hatch meeting.

also fitted in conjunction with the head gaskets, the former a modification already employed to help prevent gasket failure and one which should have been an omen of the problems that now arose.

For the start of the race, which was to be the Aston V8's first proper endurance run, Surtees lined up in the long-tailed car in 11th spot on the grid. His race, though, was doomed to be short, the still overheating SL73/121 retiring on the third lap with a holed piston after just 59 minutes, albeit after Surtees had pushed the car into eighth place. SL73/101 fared little better, its troubles beginning seven laps later when the fuel injection pump began to overheat and seize due to a fractured camshaft drive. The latter was replaced, but a lap later the Irwin/de Klerk machine was back in the pits to have the camshaft pulley tightened. It then ran for a while without problems until at 2 hours 32 minutes into the race, accompanied by a drop in oil pressure, the crankshaft damper exploded and the Lola-Aston Martin effort was well and truly over.

Between practice and the race, as a precautionary measure

Aston's mechanics had increased the dimensions of the Cooper seal rings beneath the V8's cylinder heads to further reduce its tendency to overheat. While this may have been a good thing on SL73/101, on the Surtees/Hobbs car it made little difference because it was only realized after the event that the different aerodynamics and longer tail of this car were the main cause of its overheating. It was also felt that SL73/101's V8 had not been helped by Surtees' insistence on using a brand of spark plug not previously tried on the racing Aston engine.

More importantly, further investigation at Newport Pagnell revealed twisted blocks and misaligned bearing caps, highlighting serious weaknesses in the V8's crankcase rigidity. Moreover, there was again evidence of cracking around the main bearing housing, a problem believed to have been cured in the initial development stages of the V8. This discovery once again proved the worth of motor racing because no such problems had arisen during road tests of the new V8 engine.

To get to the root of the problem the engine from

The engine in this development DBS V8, in fact a converted DBS, was a Lola-Aston 5-litre unit fitted with downdraught IDA Webers and carrying a suitable bonnet bulge.

SL73/121 was rebuilt with just the holed piston, one other piston and an exhaust valve being replaced. After two days running-in on the bench, the alloy V8 was subjected to a full endurance run, and this time the engine lasted for 27½ hours before block cracking became evident. From the nature and location of the cracks it was realized that the main bearing studs were putting their inherent lateral forces back into the main bearing housing rather than the block walls, perhaps exacerbated by the larger main bearing caps latterly fitted to the V8. Accordingly, the engine's bottom end was modified with additional buttressing or webbing and with this new type of block the V8 was run for two separate 25-hour endurance tests, after each of which no signs of cracking could be found.

It was thus two years after the V8's debut in the Lola-Aston Martin at Nürburgring that Aston Martin felt that its new engine was finally ready for installation in a production car, namely the DBS V8. Extensive testing had been undertaken with a prototype DBS V8, actually a converted DBS, using a downdraught carburettor version of the Lola-Aston engine in 5-litre form. From its original Marek design, the all-alloy V8 had benefited from considerable strengthening, much of this internal redesign being overseen by Alan Crouch, who was to succeed Tadek Marek, having previously worked with him on the V8. There were also a few additional modifications, such as an increase in capacity to 5,340cc using a bore of 100mm and a stroke of 85mm, pistons with reduced 'slap', a lower-capacity oil pump and Bosch, rather than AE Brico, fuel injection, the feeling being that the German system offered the better compromise in terms of overall performance and US Federal emission regulations. Thus equipped, and in no small way due to the efforts of the Lola-Aston Martins on the track, the Aston Martin DBS V8 was able to boast both a very strong engine and an impressive power output of 320bhp @ 5,000rpm and almost 360lb/ft of torque. A Vantage version had already been mooted at this time, one V8 having been equipped with downdraught IDA Webers and DB4 GT high-lift camshafts, and producing almost 400bhp. However, it would be a considerable time before such a Vantage-engined production Aston Martin became available.

CHAPTER 3

The DBS V8

A new supercar is born

The DBS was launched in 1967 with the same 4-litre twin-overhead-camshaft engine and five-speed ZF transmission as used in the DB6, the Mk2 version of which initially ran concurrently in production alongside the new model. It had always been planned that the William Towns-designed DBS would be the first Aston to use the new V8, but the production problems recounted in the previous chapters contributed to the delay of such a marriage. It was not until September 27, 1969, after three DBS models had completed exhaustive tests with the 5-litre version of the V8, that the DBS V8 model was finally announced.

The DBS had rather unfairly been slated as something of a lethargic performer, particularly in automatic, non-Vantage guise, due to its six-cylinder engine having to carry an extra 3cwt (more than 150kg) over the DB6, though the top speed of over 140mph and 0 to 60 and 0 to 100mph acceleration times of 7.1 and 18.0 seconds respectively recorded by *Motor*, with Michael Bowler (later to become a director of Proteus Technology, Aston Martin's racing wing) at the wheel, were not to be sniffed at in late 1967. Strangely, although it used the very same DBS Vantage with manual gearchange, *Autocar*'s figures were considerably poorer, 8.6 and 19.6 seconds being recorded for the two acceleration times, and unfortunately those were the figures, which were recorded in less favourable weather conditions, that most people tended to remember. With a 50/50 weight distribution and all-new de Dion rear suspension – allowing inboard rear discs – allied to the traditional front wishbone set-up, the DBS was a very safe handling car with superb balance and brakes to match.

Indeed, *Motor* headlined its road test "S for 'superb'".

The DBS thus provided an excellent first home for Marek's 5.34-litre V8 engine, which fitted snugly into the front compartment. At the time of the DBS V8's launch, Aston Martin was not in the habit of releasing power and torque figures as it was still wincing from exaggerated American bhp claims. However, we now know that the early DBS V8 cars produced around 320bhp at 5,000rpm and 360lb/ft of torque – and it had certainly been calculated within the factory that at least 300bhp would be needed for the heavier DBS V8 just to match the performance of the 280bhp (325bhp claimed) Vantage-engined DB6, which had been clocked at 6.1 seconds to 60mph and 15.0 seconds to 100mph. Very few modifications were made to accommodate the all-alloy V8 motor and the increased power, yet the DBS V8 retained nearly all DBS's virtues intact, while performance in early 1970 was nothing short of staggering with 0 to 60mph recorded by *Motor* in just 5.9 seconds, 0 to 100mph in 13.8 seconds and a top speed of 160.4mph (*Autocar* figures this time were far more comparable at 6.0sec to 60mph and a 161.5mph maximum, though the 0 to 100mph time was almost a second slower at 14.7 seconds).

The only visual differences between the DBS and DBS V8 (please will people stop creating the 'DBS6', a non-existent model – by definition, a DBS is a six-cylinder car) were a deeper front air dam and specially produced 7 x 15in alloy wheels, compared to the DBS's weaker 6 x 15in wire-spoked wheels, which it was felt might not be man enough to handle the V8's torque. The similarity to the eye between the two

The William Towns-designed DBS had clean and elegant lines and ample room under the bonnet for the eagerly awaited Aston V8 engine.

Fitting Marek's 5.34-litre V8 to the DBS resulted in 160mph performance, making the DBS V8 one of the fastest cars in the world.

Visually the DBS V8 was identical to the 4-litre DBS bar wider alloy wheels and tyres and different badging.

The DBS V8 was equipped with Girling ventilated disc brakes front and rear, operated through independent hydraulic circuits. The swept area was 259sq in at the front and 209sq in at the rear. Separate calipers on the rear discs were provided for the fly-off handbrake.

models was amply demonstrated by the televison series *The Persuaders* in which Roger Moore apparently drove a DBS V8 (and Tony Curtis a Ferrari Dino 246). The car was, in fact, a DBS (chassis no DBS/5636/R) but as the DBS V8 had recently been launched, Aston Martin was keen that its new, but as yet unavailable, flagship should be given exposure and the DBS accordingly had its hubs and wheels changed to resemble a DBS V8.

Under the skin there were also a few changes to the DBS V8. To handle the extra power, 10.75 x 1.25in ventilated discs were fitted at the front and 10.38 x 1.25in at the rear, as against the DBS's solid 11.46in and 10.37in diameter items, while spring rates were increased to cope with the extra weight of around 55lb. In addition, the five-speed ZF transmission had revised ratios allied to a 3.54:1 axle ratio with a 3.33:1 option, the latter being standard when, as was usually the case, the new and already popular Chrysler Torqueflite automatic gearbox was fitted, as opposed to the previous models' Borg-Warner unit.

Road test reports on the new DBS V8 were most

18

A factory shot of the DBS V8 at Forbes House, home of the Society of Motor Manufacturers and Traders, in London's Belgravia.

Another view of the car at Forbes House.

favourable, which was not surprising as at the time it was one of the fastest production cars in the world, and certainly the fastest with a full four-seat capacity. The extra weight over the DBS did slightly reduce the car's balance over its six-cylinder brother, while in the wet the wider Pirelli tyres did not provide the same high level of adhesion as the DBS's narrower, but similarly 70-profile Avons. Some testers also complained of poor torque at low revs – a minor criticism in relation to the Aston's overall performance and one which, anyway, was removed as the model was gradually developed.

American buyers, representing Aston Martin's largest market outside Britain, were not able to get their hands on the DBS V8 until 18 months after its European launch, the interim time being necessary to finalize its specification to meet the strict federal emission regulations. Mechanical changes included a reduced compression ratio and air injection in order to keep hydrocarbon and carbon monoxide

It wasn't long before the DBS V8 appeared in club sprints and hillclimbs. Here one uses its considerable performance to storm through the Esses at an AMOC Wiscombe Park hillclimb.

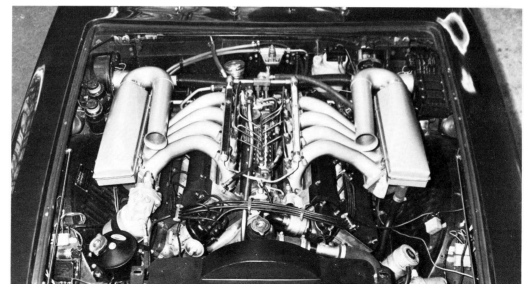

A neat piece of packaging showing the 5,340cc engine installed in the front of a DBS V8. The Bosch fuel injection is being fed by individual ram pipes from balanced throttle control boxes with large micronic air filters.

AMOC member John Cope's concours-winning DBS V8 looking magnificent at Greenwich.

emissions to the required minimum, with a resultant inevitable drop in power output and thus performance. An unfortunate side-effect of the delay in American exports was a lack of interest in concurrent Aston models, once the more powerful DBS V8 had been announced, despite the lengthy wait for exports to the USA. It also meant that by the time the DBS V8 was available in the USA in October 1971, just two months remained before revised, and even stricter, emission regulations came into force.

Production of the DBS V8 had begun in April 1970 (alongside the DB6 Mk2 and DBS) with chassis number DBSV8/10001/R, and while the model was being 'emissionized' for the USA, work was already underway in the wind-tunnel to enhance its aerodynamics for a Series 2 version. However, no revised or new models – bar the stretched four-door Lagonda version of the DBS V8 – were

destined to see the light of day under Sir David Brown's tenure of the company, any development being hindered by the unfortunate financial state of Aston Martin Lagonda Limited. The man who had held the reins at Newport Pagnell so well, and had so effectively put the marque back on the motorsport map, felt that too much money was being lost to justify continuing and thus he sold the company on February 16, 1972. The purchaser (for a claimed mere £100) was Company Developments, which effectively took control from the David Brown Corporation in April the same year, and was chosen because of a declared desire to see Aston Martin Lagonda prosper. Production of the DBS V8 ceased the following month with chassis number DBSV8/10405/RCA and while Series 2 versions replaced both it and the DBS, the company was soon again in financial trouble.

CHAPTER 4

V8 metamorphosis

Series 2 to 5 and Volante

The wind-tunnel work conducted on the DBS V8 during 1971 had resulted in a revised body shape, again courtesy of William Towns. Designated MP 231, it featured single headlights, a revised radiator grille and a less sloping rear screen/roof treatment that ended on a higher and heavier boot line – in fact, the rear looked like a cross between that of a Maserati Ghibli and a Ford Mustang Mach 1. Fortunately, this revised rear was not adopted and in effect only the nose of MP 231 was incorporated to change the DBS V8's external appearance – increasing its length by 2½in and making the front reminiscent of the famous DB3S and DB MkIII models – and transforming it into what would be called simply the Aston Martin V8. This new model went into production in May 1972, beginning with chassis number V8/10501/RCA, alongside the Aston Martin Vantage, which was basically a DBS with a Vantage-tune engine as standard and also featured the single-headlamp treatment (but with 7in quartz iodine lamps as opposed to the DBS/DBS V8's double 5½in units). From the outset, Company Developments, under the chairmanship of William Wilson, had decided to drop the DB prefix to model numbering and thus the DBS and DBS V8 models became the very last of the David Brown Aston Martins.

With the change from DBS V8 to AM V8 came other notable revisions such as improved sound-deadening and heat insulation between engine and bulkhead, transistorized Lucas Opus ignition, revised induction air boxes and a spare wheel laid flat in the boot to increase luggage capacity. The 3.33:1 and 2.88:1 rear axle ratios (the latter previously an

option with automatic transmission), became standard for manual and automatic cars respectively, while the traditional wood-rim steering wheel had already been dropped on the last DBS V8 models in preference for one with a thicker, leather rim. The last DBS V8s were fitted with air conditioning as standard and this was carried over to the new model. The price for the AM V8 was now £8,750 compared to £6,900 for the first DBS V8 and it would soon rise again.

During 1971 it had been discovered that the V8 production engines were delivering a little under 300bhp, well below the 320bhp of the first models, and that problems would occur in suitably recalibrating the Bosch injection to meet the latest US Federal emission laws. Various Weber carburettor set-ups were tried once more to overcome both problems, including fitment of sidedraught 45 DCOE and downdraught 48 IDA and 42 DCNF units, while turbocharging was also considered as a possibility after experiments carried out by Aston Martin Lagonda Incorporated, AML's American arm. Ultimately it was the DCNF type that was chosen as the best compromise, but a lack of finance meant that incorporating such a specification had to be temporarily shelved, despite being cheaper and easier to maintain than the injection system. It was left to Company Developments to revitalize this carburettor version and this it did in the form of another revised AM V8 in August 1973. Production of the Series 2 AM V8 had lasted just 15 months and it ended with chassis number V8/10789/RCA (the Aston Martin Vantage – the last of the six-cylinder Astons – ended its run at the same time) and

22

An AM V8 Series 2 takes a tight line through Bunnie's Leap at the Wiscombe Park hillclimb. This second fuel-injection model, and the first V8 car with single headlights, was in production for only three months in 1972.

Series 3 models began with chassis number V8/11002/RCA.

The fitment of the four twin-choke Webers necessitated a larger bonnet bulge, which for the first time extended to the edge of the bonnet, while the ventilation louvres between the rear window and bootlid disappeared in favour of a more attractive lip. The carburettor engine offered increased low and mid-range torque, removing a criticism of the fuel-injected V8, with improved throttle response and none of the injected engine's tendency to hunt at idle. There was also the bonus of an improvement in average fuel consumption of almost 2mpg to 14–15mpg – depending, of course, on the weight of one's right foot, which is often a problem with an Aston Martin! Engine and transmission cooling were also improved and a 3.07:1 axle ratio became an option for automatic-transmission cars and the old 3.54:1 ratio became an alternative for cars with the manual five-speed ZF gearbox. The Pirelli tyres, meanwhile, were dropped in favour of similarly-sized Avons.

Inside the Series 3 V8 there were detail changes such as revised switchgear, a larger ashtray, improved seats, fuses located in the glove box and 'central locking' for the passenger door, while sound and heat insulation between the

The major change to the Series 3 AM V8 was the fitment of quadruple Weber carburettors in place of the Bosch fuel injection, necessitating a larger bonnet bulge and air intake than previously.

engine/transmission and passenger compartment was further increased. It was particularly important to Aston Martin's survival abroad that more people should find themselves attracted into a V8's Connolly hide and Wilton carpet-equipped interior, and the carburettor engine allowed suitable adjustments to be made to meet the latest US and Japanese emission laws, those in the US being met officially from October 1974.

Contemporary road test figures show that the fitment of carburettors either did or did not make a notable difference to the performance of the AM V8, depending on whose figures one chose to accept. *Autocar*, in September 1973, recorded a rapid 6.2 seconds from 0 to 60mph, but with a top speed well down at 146mph against the DBS V8's 160mph

(the similarly fuel-injected Series 2 AM V8 was never tested). On the other hand, *Motor*, during the same week, achieved a 155mph maximum, 5mph down on its DBS V8 figure, and a 0 to 60mph acceleration time of just 5.7 seconds, 0.2sec faster than the DBS V8.

At the time, though, such disparity of performance figures was of little significance to Aston Martin Lagonda, which once again was in dire financial straits, and not being helped by high oil prices, its products' still high thirst for fuel, and the expense of making the V8 conform to US emission regulations. In January 1974, Company Developments applied to the Department of Trade and Industry under the Industries Act to borrow £500,000 capital through the banks, but was unable to negotiate a suitable loan. The Department

The extra height of the carburated engine is evident in this shot.

An AM V8 Series 3 in the service department at Newport Pagnell with non-standard driving lamps. Note the rare DB6 Shooting Brake in the background.

George Abecassis, one-time works Aston Martin driver, hands over the keys of the 1,000th Aston production car. Managing director Alan Curtis is on the left.

Getting a move on at an AMOC Curborough sprint – this is a Series 3 car, distinguishable by single headlights and large bonnet air intake.

also decreed that sourcing such funding through the private sector would not meet the requirements of the Industries Act and suggested that the factory should make a fresh application. This was duly done, but again it was refused.

Aston Martin's predicament came firmly into the public eye during September 1974 when, during pre-election campaigning, an MP declared that unless the Trade and Industry Secretary (then Anthony Wedgewood Benn) intervened, Aston Martin would collapse. But the appeal fell on deaf ears, as did another application by Company Developments after the election, and Aston Martin was forced into receivership on December 30, 1974, car production coming to a halt the following day. Nonetheless, the company had still managed to show the new Aston Martin Lagonda at the October Earls Court Motor Show, five years after David Brown had seen the first prototype built on a stretched DBS chassis.

Ironically, this sad state of affairs ultimately created a 'Catch 22' situation – a contract for 200 cars per year had been forthcoming from the USA if the cars met current emission regulations (which they did from October 1974) and if Government assistance for the company was guaranteed. Unfortunately, the Labour Government agreed such support only if the USA contract was secured first! Sadly, Governmental indifference to such an established piece of British motoring heritage did not come as a complete surprise, and it seemed that Aston Martin was destined to oblivion.

With receivership came 450 redundancies at the Newport Pagnell factory, a small skeleton staff under the Receiver and sales manager Fred Hartley being left to run the company while a buyer was sought. Prospects for Aston Martin were indeed looking gloomy until an offer by two businessmen, American entrepreneur Peter Sprague and Canadian sports car dealer George Minden, both of whom were members of the Aston Martin Owners Club, was accepted on June 27, 1975. Between them they put up £1.05 million in equity and the company was renamed Aston Martin Lagonda (1975) Limited. With the election of Alan Curtis (who had earlier bid for the company) and Denis Flather to the Board the following January, more cash was forthcoming and Aston Martin Lagonda looked to be once more on a firm footing. Fred Hartley was appointed managing director, Harold Beach remained consultant, Mike Loasby returned to the fold after some years away and engine man Dave Morgan also rejoined. Staff numbers were duly increased, including many who had been made redundant, and by mid-1976 production was back to almost six cars per week, the same output as three years earlier.

Of the new management quartet, it was Alan Curtis who proved to have the best combination of vision and business acumen and once production was rolling again in the spring of 1976 it was not long before new and revised models were being planned. Curtis felt that the V8 was already showing its age and there were suggestions of an all-new model for 1978, while the radical design of the new Lagonda Series 2 had

already been started by William Towns.

To pep up the existing V8, two stages of engine tune were developed. The more powerful of these, Stage 2, offered a 40% power increase and was destined for the superb V8 Vantage launched in February 1977 (and dealt with later), while Stage 1 was reserved for 'ordinary' V8s. By the time the latter was standardized in June 1977, ever tightening emission regulations in Europe and the USA had seen the Aston V8's power output stifled back to around 280bhp. Effectively, Stage 1 replaced the missing horses, restoring output to a regular 304bhp at 5,500rpm, the power curve peaking 500rpm higher than previously. Detail changes included the adoption of different camshaft profiles, which helped to reduce noise, and the exhaust system from the V8 Vantage.

The following year, however, the specification was changed again with the introduction in October 1978 of the Series 4 V8, commonly known as 'Oscar India' (in deference to Curtis' love of aviation). Series 3 production ceased with chassis number V8/12031/RCA and a different system of chassis

Aston Martin Lagonda has traditionally supplied the pace car at AMOC competition events. Here a new Series 4 'Oscar India' V8 is on duty at Wiscombe Park. Note built-in tail spoiler. Driving lamps within the radiator intake were a popular fitment.

numbering was introduced for Series 4 cars, beginning with V8SOR 12032 – S denoting S1 engine tune. This model was easily distinguishable by its built-in rear boot spoiler, similar to that of the V8 Vantage, as was a redesigned bonnet without air intake which had also appeared on the convertible V8 Volante in June the same year. Underneath, shock absorber settings were revised – the old Armstrong Selectarides had already been dropped a few years earlier – and the exhaust system was fabricated in stainless steel for the first time.

The Series 4 was substantially restyled inside, the most notable change being the use of wood veneer for both the dashboard and the doors as had first been seen on the V8 Volante. The cloth roof lining was replaced by leather, there were restyled headrests, a new centre console provided a cigarette lighter for rear passengers, and the air conditioning was improved.

Changes to the V8 engine followed in June 1980 and included larger and Tuftrided dished valves, polynomial camshaft profiles, smaller cylinder head porting standardized with the Vantage, barrel-shaped pistons and a compression

The car looked cleaner, however, without them. This is Roger Kohn's example, also seen on the front cover. The central badge is the AMOC's motif.

A Series 4 V8 was used to good effect on the 1979 Grosvenor House Beaujolais Run. This is the winning car outside London's Cafe Royal.

ratio increased from 9.0 to 9.3:1, the same as that of the Vantage, which was simultaneously reduced from 9.5:1 (though engines destined for the USA had the ratio reduced from 8.5 to 8.0:1 to meet yet stricter emission laws). The engine numbering code was also changed, the familiar V/540, denoting the engine's capacity, being changed to V/580 in deference to the year.

Power output was said to be the same as previously with a slight increase in torque and better fuel economy, but road test reports of the time show that the Aston Martin V8 in its latest guise was noticeably slower than before. Both *Autocar* and *Motor* could manage no better than 7.2 seconds for the 0 to 60mph dash, while maximum speed was down to 145mph, 15mph less than the original DBS V8. It was generally agreed, however, that the Series 4's level of refinement was an improvement over previous series which, along with the loss of performance and an increase in price from £23,000 (in 1978) to £34,500 (in 1980), tended to relegate the model to

a smaller market of buyers who perhaps did not hold outright performance as a high priority. Nevertheless, there appeared to be no shortage of customers following the car's introduction at the 1978 Birmingham Motor Show.

Also on display there was the all-new V8 Volante, which had been launched five months earlier on June 21. The Volante moniker had first been used on convertible DB6 models (previous open models were called either Drophead Coupés or Convertibles, the latter name being applicable to the DB4 and DB5). Once the US regulations restricting production of open cars had been eased, and Aston's financial situation had improved sufficiently to make development of such a model feasible, American dealers, operating through a new importer appointed in 1976, had been quick to request a convertible version of the V8. Work began on the model under Harold Beach in 1977, and conversion from the fixed-head car proved to be fairly straightforward once some initial scuttle shake had been eliminated by fitting a rear underbody

The Series 4's interior featured wood veneer for the dashboard, door trims and centre console for the first time on the Saloon.

The Americans were the first to get their hands on the V8 Volante, launched in June 1978. On the right is a DB6 Volante and behind a DBS. The AMOC's Rosi Aslett is standing with the new car.

subframe (rumour has it that its shape was inspired by a garden gate!). Naturally, additional strengthening was required to compensate for the lack of a roof and, like the later V8 Vantage Zagato, torsional rigidity was around 15% greater than in the roofed car from which it originated. There were thus no worries regarding the £33,864 car's safety in the event of a crash, while a novel safety feature of another kind was a sensor connected to the handbrake lever that prevented the hood from being lowered unless the car was at a standstill. Production officially began during June 1986, beginning with chassis number V8COR 15001.

The V8 Volante was well received all round, particularly by the Americans who had requested it, of course, and over a year was to pass before any UK or European buyers were able to get their hands on one. Internally, the Volante was the same as the V8 Saloon (yes, that is what Aston call the closed V8!) with the addition of walnut burr for the dashboard and door cappings, a feature for which the V8 had to wait until it appeared in Series 4 guise at Birmingham. Similarly, the Volante was ahead of the Series 4 in having its bonnet air intake blanked off (sharing this with the 1977 V8 Vantage), though the latter's boot spoiler was not adopted, and naturally the hood was power-operated, stowing neatly away behind the rear seats without intruding on the car's interior space. Its positioning did reduce boot capacity somewhat, but this was a minor penalty for a car that looked so

The new V8 Volante during a demonstration run at the AMOC's St John Horsfall meeting at Silverstone in June 1978.

attractive, whether the hood was up or down, and after all, there had not been much room in the rear to start with!

At 4ft 6in to the top of the hood, the V8 Volante was 1¾in taller than the Saloon, while at 3,950lb its weight was 150lb greater (although the car's spring rates remained the same as for the V8 Saloon), the additional weight and wind resistance contributing to a reduction in top speed to around 140mph – nobody seems to have recorded the maximum. The factory, however, would only quote 130mph, the figure it considered to be the safe maximum for the hood mechanism; it added the recommendation that should an owner wish to exceed this figure, he or she should do so with the hood down. *Motor*, however, on March 3, 1978, reported a 0 to 60mph acceleration time of 7.7 seconds and 17.3 seconds for 0 to 100mph, performance figures considerably down on those for the V8 Saloon, although the magazine did point out that a carburation flatspot had marred the Aston's ability to pull cleanly off the mark.

Some customers requested a complete Vantage specification for their V8 Volante and, although officially the

factory refused to comply, a handful did slip off the production line. With these, of course, worries about top speed with the hood in place became more serious and I remember an instance of someone who bought such a Vantage-equipped Volante from its first owner, who stressed that 130mph should not be exceeded in closed form. The new owner, however, wishing to impress a pair of female companions on a trip to France, took the Aston up to 160mph, whereupon the beautiful hood was suddenly torn asunder! At the time, the V8 Vantage Volante, suitably re-engineered to cope with the Vantage performance, was still some years away.

In 1980 additional creature comforts were introduced to the V8 range such as central locking for both doors, gas struts for the bonnet, interior switches for the boot lock and petrol filler cap flaps, a lamp failure warning light and electrically adjusted mirrors, while cruise control became an option for cars with the automatic transmission, which now featured a lock-up facility. Sales, however, were down to half those of the previous year, though the American market, where the V8

Victor Gauntlett at the 1986 Birmingham Motor Show with the Aston Martin Junior, a scale model powered by a single-cylinder Honda engine. It featured Connolly hide, Wilton carpeting, a stereo and all the usual Aston creature comforts. Note the V8 Vantage Zagato in the background.

With big brother – one for father, one for son!

Volante continued to prove a popular choice, remained reasonably healthy.

Alan Curtis felt that the best method of offsetting the resultant financial losses was to cut production to one car a week, but there were some new shareholders who disagreed. Peter Cadbury had joined in January 1980, then in May he was followed by Victor Gauntlett with his Pace Petroleum company and Tim Hearley, representing CH Industrials. Gauntlett and Hearley were against cutting production and as a result of this disagreement Pace and CH Industrials bought out the other shareholders in January 1981. With the departure of Alan Curtis (he would later take over the helm at Lotus) and the others the company was renamed simply Aston Martin Lagonda Limited. Attention was then turned to America, where the Lagonda had yet to meet forthcoming emission laws, and the Middle East, where the Lagonda proved to be an absolute winner, helping to increase 1980 sales by 25 cars in 1981. Meanwhile, Aston Martin Tickford had also been busy with conversions such as the Frazer Tickford Metro, the turbocharged Tickford Capri (which

HRH Prince Charles, a long-time Aston owner (he owns a DB6 Mk 2 Volante and a V8 Vantage Volante) inspects a Junior with Victor Gauntlett.

At AML's Cheval Place, London showroom, two children pose in a Junior. Actor Ian Ogilvy has just handed over the keys to the NSPCC for a charity auction – by now the Junior cost £12,500.

This shot of a Junior dwarfed by a Lagonda shows just how small it really is. At least one publication captioned a handout shot as a V8 Volante!

was to be sold by Ford, marking an early association between the two companies), Jaguar's XJ-S Cabriolet and development of a race version of the V8 for use in the Nimrod-Aston Martins that were to compete in the World Endurance Championship the following year.

The financial climate in Britain led to a drop in demand for the Series 4 V8, but production continued nevertheless and this model was to have the longest production run of any of the DBS V8 and AM V8 series, extending to over seven years before it was superseded by the Series 5 in early 1986. Aston Martin Lagonda, however, was to face another financial crisis in 1983 when an excess of world oil supplies meant not only that Pace Petroleum faced considerable difficulties of its own, but that, having less money to spend, the Arabs were buying fewer Astons, only 28 of them compared to the 74 they had taken in 1982. Gauntlett at this time was having to spend all of his time at Pace (previously he had split his week between Pace and AML), and to add to the difficulties, there was union unrest at Newport Pagnell regarding bonuses, which led to some sackings by managing director Bill Archer.

Shortly afterwards he resigned and in July Victor Gauntlett returned full-time to the factory.

It was at about this time that Peter Livanos, of the Greek shipping family, entered the Aston Martin story via a shareholding in the American subsidiary, Aston Martin Lagonda Incorporated. The share purchase came about after he had visited the showroom to buy a used Aston, and he was to become both a devoted Aston enthusiast and a major force behind the marque. Through him the Papanicolaous brothers (also in shipping) were brought into the frame and between them they took a majority shareholding, at first in the American Aston wing and then in Aston Martin Lagonda Ltd itself. Via a company called Automotive Investments Incorporated they acquired all the Pace shares, which effectively gave them 55% of the share stock.

A condition of the sale, however, was that Victor Gauntlett would remain at Aston's helm (Ford was to make a similar condition when it purchased majority shares four years later) and he agreed to this, selling Pace Petroleum in late 1983. In some ways, the name Pace had become synonymous with

The Series 5 AM V8 is easily distinguishable by its almost flat bonnet and BBS wheels.

Under the bonnet of the Series 5 the major change was a reversion to fuel injection, this time a Weber/Marelli system. Power was now quoted as 305bhp.

Aston Martin, having been the major sponsor of both the works and the Viscount Downe-entered Nimrod-Astons during 1982, and it was a shame to see the pairing finally part company. A few months later, in early 1984, the Greek trio increased their shares further by buying out CH Industrials, at the same time increasing their stake in Aston Martin Tickford to majority status. They were also able to invest in a new and revitalized in-house engineering and development facility, its establishment being overseen by former motoring journalist and Pace director Michael Bowler (who had been responsible for all Aston Martin-related sponsorship matters at Pace and, as previously mentioned, was later to become operations director of Proteus Technology, Aston Martin's racing wing).

Production of the Series 4 V8 came to an end in 1986, coinciding with the launch at the New York Motor Show on January 25 of the Series 5; the last Series 4 car bore the chassis number V8SOR 12499. The preceding two years had witnessed a turnaround in the economic climate and sales of all Aston models had increased steadily, including the Lagonda, which was now going down well in the USA.

However, in 1984 there had been yet another crisis and change of ownership at Newport Pagnell when the volatile oil market affected the Livanos and Papanicolaou shipping interests, hitting cash-flow hard. As a result the Papanicolaou shares were acquired by the Livanos family, giving them a controlling 75% interest, while Victor Gauntlett bought the remaining 25% of the company. At the same time, production was cut from five to four cars per week with some inevitable redundancies. As had become customary at Newport Pagnell, AML – which had been renamed again to Aston Martin Lagonda Group Limited – was to come out of the latest crisis on top and by the time production of the Series 5 began, weekly output had risen again to five cars per week.

The most notable difference in the latest V8 was the reversion to fuel injection, though this time a Weber/Marelli rather than a Bosch system was employed; the change also marked a return to the flat bonnet without the scoop which had been necessary to clear the carburettors. The new model also used 8in wide BBS alloy wheels which had been standardized on the Series 4 V8 Saloon and Series 1 V8

This one-off long-wheelbase Series 5 V8 was specially lengthened by Aston Martin from new at a customer's request. The combination of an extra 7 inches and low-profile tyres, however, strikes an odd balance, but AML will usually accommodate a customer's needs – at a cost!

Simultaneously launched with the Series 5 V8 was the Series 2 V8 Volante, incorporating similar changes. This is Victor Gauntlett's own car. Note the BBS wheels and 'flat' bonnet.

A V8 Vantage Volante became available for the first time in October 1986. Its body accoutrements, however, were not to everyone's taste.

The V8 Vantage Volante at its show launch at the NEC.

These two V8 Vantage Volantes make a handsome pair of one of the world's fastest convertibles.

Volante during 1983 (when the air conditioning was uprated for the second time) and its length had crept up a fraction to 15ft 4in. Compared to the original DBS V8 it was 3¾in longer and 202lb heavier. For the first time in many years Aston Martin quoted a power output, this time 305bhp at 5,000rpm (the power peak being down by 500rpm again) with 320lb/ft of torque; by this time declaration of output had become a requirement under German import legislation. The specification was otherwise much the same as for the Series 4 apart from a new 3.058:1 axle ratio for cars with automatic transmission, and Newport Pagnell quoted a top speed of 150mph and acceleration from 0 to 60mph in 6.7 seconds, a notable improvement. Chassis and engine number coding was again revised, the former from V8SOR to V8SGR, and the latter from V580 to V585 (the 85 denoting the year), thus the first Series 5 off the line was chassis V8SGR 12500.

Understandably, all the improvements of the Series 5 were passed on to the V8 Volante, which became the Series 2 model at the same time, beginning with chassis V8CGL 15440; the last Series 1 car carried the chassis number V8CFR 15439. Interestingly, the V8 Volante's weight was now quoted at 4,009lb, exactly the same as the current V8 Saloon, while the price had risen to £68,500. A little over a year later, in May 1987, the Volante's plastic rear window was replaced by glass, a modification that did not help storage and spoilt somewhat the 'hood-up' lines of the model. An additional hood fastener was now also connected to the central locking. In October 1986, customers who had wanted to buy a proper Vantage version of the Volante could finally do so with the launch of the V8 Vantage Volante. Some, however, were not over-enamoured with the modified body, which featured wide side skirts blending in with arches which were wider than those of the V8 Vantage Saloon, as well as a front air dam, bootlid spoiler and rear valance – clearly it is a matter of taste. The new model, priced at £93,500, incorporated all the changes of the Series 3 V8 Vantage, including the latest 400bhp engine, with the option of the 432bhp version first seen in the V8 Vantage Zagato and 16in x 8in BBS alloy wheels. Again, no full performance figures appear to be available, but the factory's claim of performance being on a par with that of the V8 Vantage Saloon seems justifiable.

For many years there had been talk of a new Aston Martin model to replace the V8, but each time the subject was raised the existing car was given a new lease of life, either through the introduction of updates and revisions or because of a sudden increase in demand. However, the end of the road for the V8 finally came into sight with the launch of the all-new Virage at the 1988 Birmingham Motor Show. Delays with tooling and other hiccups contrived to delay deliveries of the first Virages to the many customers who had eagerly placed deposits, and this effectively gave the V8 a temporary stay of execution, but the end finally came in December 1989 when the very last chassis, V8VKR 12701, rolled off the line. The classic design of the DBS V8 and V8 models had endured for 20 years, but the Virage is a most suitable motor to take on the mantle of Britain's – and many would say the world's – most painstakingly built supercar.

CHAPTER 5

Aston Martin Lagonda

Series 1, 2 and 3

Following David Brown's takeover of the ailing Lagonda company in 1947, 10 years would elapse before production of Lagondas (with coachwork by Tickford, another company acquired by DB) ceased, only to begin again with the DB4-based 4-litre Rapide model, of which 55 were produced between 1961 and 1964. The Lagonda name as an individual model type was then to lie dormant for another five years until a unique four-door Aston Martin Lagonda DBS V8 was specially produced for (by then, Sir) David Brown's personal use in 1969.

Quite simply, this was a prototype stretched DBS fitted with the V8 engine, resulting in a wheelbase 12in longer than normal and a total length of 15ft 10¾in. To increase torsional rigidity the chassis side-members featured additional bolstering and initially the car retained the DBS's brakes and wire wheels, but soon these were to be changed to the production components of the shortly to be launched DBS V8, namely alloy wheels and ventilated disc brakes. David Brown would have liked to have seen this Aston Martin Lagonda (prototype chassis number MP 230), which was the first model to bear the joint name, put into production as well, but resources were better directed towards Aston Martin models. It was not to be until August 1974, nearly three years after David Brown had sold out to Company Developments, that the Lagonda model was revitalized, this time bearing the single-headlight frontal treatment of the AM V8 and a distinctive Lagonda radiator grille, rather than the Lagonda DBS V8's simple change of badge.

Apart from offering four doors, the Lagonda V8 boasted cosmic fire-finish paintwork and headlamp wipers as standard equipment over normal Aston specification. At 4,400lb it was also 600lb heavier than the Aston V8, though the fuel tank for this presumably thirstier car was actually a gallon smaller at 20 gallons. Other than an increased length to 16ft 2in, now 10¼in longer than the V8, all other dimensions were the same as the Aston.

Launched at the 1974 Earls Court Motor Show at a total price of £14,040, £2,691 more expensive than the contemporary V8, this first production Aston Martin Lagonda V8 was a calculated gamble designed to widen Aston Martin's appeal at a time when the financial situation at Newport Pagnell was decidedly shaky. Sadly, it was far from a sure bet and demand was such that only seven cars were built (two of which had manual gearboxes) before production ceased in June 1976; the short run began with chassis number L/12001/RCAC and ended with L/12007/RCAC.

Four months before production of these Lagondas had ceased, however, William Towns had already started drawing up a very different Series 2 version. With a platform chassis designed by Mike Loasby, incorporating the Aston Martin V8's suspension – but with self-levelling rear dampers – and steering, the result was to be quite radical in its design, as much internally as externally with its innovative digital instrumentation via cathode-ray tubes, also courtesy of Loasby in conjunction with the Cranfield Institute. Appropriately launched at Aston Clinton, Buckinghamshire (from whence the Aston part of Lionel Martin's company

The DB4-based Lagonda Rapide, the last Lagonda production model under Sir David Brown's tenure of Aston Martin Lagonda.

This is the prototype four-door V8 Lagonda, based on a DBS converted to DBS V8 specification, but with a prototype 5-litre engine.

The production V8 Lagonda of which just seven were made was a stylish machine that deserved a longer lease of life.

This is one of the seven V8 Lagondas outside Proteus Technology, Aston's now defunct racing wing. Team manager Richard Williams had the rear of his car converted to 'Oscar India' specification, which suits its proportions well.

Actor Tony Curtis tries a V8 Lagonda for size. Note the shorter front door.

name was poached in deference to his hillclimbing activities there) on October 12, 1976, its sleek, sharp, straight-edge, and undoubtedly futuristic design proved to be a real crowd-puller and gave the financially troubled company a much needed fillip. It was also no mean achievement to produce such a brand new car from the drawing-board in just over seven months.

Towns' design was dictated very much by a combination of aerodynamic requirements and the desire to produce a four-door car with a separate boot, but without any unsightly heaviness at the extremities of its considerable length. Certainly, Towns achieved his aims and at 17ft 4in it was one of the longest production cars produced in Europe, although it was both ½in narrower and 1in lower than the Aston Martin V8, and rear seat room was not as generous as the design might suggest. Interestingly, the Lagonda's weight was somewhat dubiously claimed to be the same at 3,800lb as the Aston Martin V8 with which it shared all its mechanical components, albeit with the V8 engine (using milder camshafts and larger valves than in the Aston) said to be detuned to give 280bhp in the interests of flexibility and smoothness, although it is known that the smaller airbox required to clear the bonnet robbed the V8 of some power. The Chrysler Torqueflite transmission was retained – there

The all-new V8 Lagonda Series 2 at its launch in October 1976. Left to right are Fred Hartley, Denis Flather, George Minden, and Alan Curtis.

was no manual option – though the Lagonda's limited-slip differential housed a new 3.07:1 ratio. Wheels were similarly sized to the V8, but were in steel rather than alloy and fitted with stainless steel hub caps so designed as to direct cooling air to the brakes.

But while the advanced electronic dashboard with its digital readouts and touch-switch operation caused a sensation, it also required complicated circuitry and wiring, and it was soon evident that locating a supplier capable of developing the necessary electronics was going to be a

47

With its high-tech switchgear and luxurious interior, the new 145mph V8 Lagonda was an impressive machine. Its electronics, however, caused more than a few headaches.

The razor-edge design of the V8 Lagonda Series 2 was striking and certainly distinctive.

The Series 2 Lagonda's interior looked quite simple and neat on the surface. Note the single-arm steering wheel.

problem. Originally, it had been intended that a solid-state display would provide such information as average speeds and fuel consumption, speed-related consumption, indeed, all the facilities that many far more mundane modern cars now boast as standard equipment and not dissimilar to the functions of the system fitted to the new Virage. The idea was that every operation, whether it concerned simply the four pop-up headlamps or the automatic transmission (which included a lock-out facility to prevent inadvertent mis-selection of too low a gear, or reverse when in forward motion) would be engaged by just touching a switch. The idea was very sophisticated for the time, but it was that multitude of switches – 20 flanked either side of a single-spoke steering wheel with a further 26 in the door – that was the major cause of production being delayed so badly that the first customer production car, chassis number LOOR 13008, was only delivered a whole year late to Lady Tavistock on

April 24, 1978, a little over a month after the Earls Court Show car had been successfully used to pass the MIRA crash tests. Unfortunately, this late delivery, at a special press ceremony, was further marred by the Lagonda's lack of motive power, Cranfield having been unable to perfect the vital computer before the big day!

The first two prototypes, incidentally, bore the chassis numbers L/13001/R and L/13002/R, while L/13003/R was used purely for jig tests. Thereafter, LOOR 13004 and 13005 were the first development cars for Europe, LOOR 13006 a USA development car and LOOR 13007 the first USA left-hand-drive development car, also the first to be fitted with fuel injection.

The considerably increased budget that developing the Series 2 Lagonda's electronics required had a marked effect on Aston Martin Lagonda's finances, despite the fact that post-launch more than 170 orders had been taken for the car,

49

The first prototype V8 Lagonda Series 2 on test near Newport Pagnell.

including a £2,000 deposit for each. By the time the Lagonda was ready for production the price had duly risen from the estimated £20,000 to around £30,000 including taxes. The bugs were finally ironed out of the Lagonda's electronic system by American Brian Refoy, head of the Dallas, Texas-based Javelina Corporation, and it was to him that development car LOOR 13007 was sent.

Production proper, therefore, with the Refoy-redesigned electronics, which thankfully dispensed with the electronic gearchange, was further delayed until late 1978 with deliveries scheduled for early 1979, a target that this time was met, beginning with chassis number LOOR 13013. All of this necessitated another increase in price by the end of 1979, though few expected to have to pay an extra £10,000, lifting the very exclusive Lagonda to £49,933 – two and a half years earlier it had been £24,570.

There do not appear to have been any full road tests conducted of these early Series 2 Lagondas, and it was not until October 1980 that both *Autocar* and *Motor* published

full performance figures. As usual, *Motor*'s figures were the better, recording the 0 to 60mph dash in 7.9 seconds against *Autocar*'s 8.8 seconds, while the respective 0 to 100mph times were 20.3 and 20.5 seconds, although for once *Autocar* logged the higher top speed at 148mph, 2mph quicker than *Motor* managed. The Lagonda was thus one of the fastest four-door saloons in the world.

Nonetheless, it was decided that more power was needed to compensate for the Lagonda's extra weight and experiments began with a twin turbocharged version. As mentioned previously, in the USA tests had been conducted in the mid-'seventies with turbochargers as a means of getting the Aston V8 engine through the emission regulations without any loss in power, but that was the closest Aston had yet come to using forced induction on a production car. The factory, however, via chief engineer Dave Morgan (who had succeeded Mike Loasby, who by then had joined De Lorean), had assisted in developing the remarkable Pope Special of AMOC member John Pope, basically a DBS V8 clothed in a

A Lagonda Series 2 at speed about to be passed by a V8 Vantage at Silverstone in 1977.

Two thoroughbreds: Red Rum and V8 Lagonda pose at Woburn Abbey in 1979.

The rear end of the Lagonda offered reasonable boot space, but rear passenger legroom could have been more generous.

Vauxhall Magnum bodyshell that competed in Special Saloon events (see next chapter). Initially, this engine remained normally aspirated, but in the quest for more power twin Garrett turbochargers were fitted. The experience gained from this was thus usefully employed on both the 700bhp Bulldog and the prototype turbocharged Lagonda.

The easy solution would have been to fit the V8 Vantage engine, possibly detuned, but that route would probably have unduly affected the Lagonda's gentlemanly character, and turbocharging seemed the route to take without upsetting the car's established manners. On a V8 engine twin turbochargers will always provide better throttle response than one, and two Garrett TO3 units were thus employed on chassis LOOR 13004, though the tight fit in the engine bay necessitated their fitment in the Lagonda's lengthy nose. In conjunction with special Cosworth pistons, reducing the compression ratio to 7.5:1, the standard 42 DCNF carburettors and a maximum boost pressure of 10psi, power

was claimed to be similar to the contemporary Aston V8 Vantage's 380bhp, though no figures were released at the time. Torque, however, was quoted as almost 500lb/ft between 3,200 and 3,500rpm, while at least 450lb/ft was said to be constantly available between 2,500 and 4,500rpm, a mammoth figure for a production car. In April 1980, *Motor* briefly road-tested this Lagonda and found it capable of considerable performance, on one occasion 'leaving an XJ-S gasping for breath', while estimating top speed as in excess of 150mph. The magazine was indeed impressed and finished its article by saying: 'Some things still make one proud to be British'. Sadly, though, the turbocharged Lagonda was never to go into production.

As with the Aston Martin V8, the Lagonda received detail changes as production continued and in September 1983, by which time the badging now simply read Lagonda (having dropped the Aston Martin prefix), BBS wheels and American specification spoilers and bumpers became standard

HRH Prince Charles test-drove a
Lagonda Series 2. Note the happy
looking bodyguard behind!

A Series 3 V8 Lagonda looking very
svelte. Note the new-style wheels
and a Virage in the background.

Prior to the Lagonda Series 3 launch, AML experimented with a twin-turbocharged version of the V8, seen here. *Motor Sport* found its performance most impressive.

Interior of the Lagonda Series 3. Note the more conventional wheel and the restyled facia with wood veneer.

A little over two years earlier, in October 1983, the Tickford Lagonda had become available. Its side skirts and spoilers were a matter of taste and looked out of keeping. Only five were sold.

equipment. One month later, a rather garish Tickford version was presented at Motorfair on October 19 in pearlescent white complete with two colour televisions; only five of these cars were sold, presumably to Middle Eastern customers who had to part with £85,000 for the privilege. By now, the standard Lagonda's price had risen to an inclusive £66,000, while a 1984 limited edition long-wheelbase version, again by Tickford – just three were sold – cost a cool £110,000.

The year 1984 also saw the introduction at the Birmingham Motor Show of multi-lingual, verbal accompaniment to the electronic, computerized dashboard displays – either English, French, German or Arabic were now available at the touch of another switch. Thereafter, the Lagonda remained little changed until the New York Show on January 25, 1986, when fuel injection was announced as standard, concurrently with the Series 5 Aston Martin V8, this change being sufficient to warrant the Lagonda model as a Series 3 version. Power had increased to 300bhp, but still delivered no more than 240bhp in USA trim. Not surprisingly, the Lagonda's weight had increased again to 4,622lb, while the rear axle ratio was now 3.058:1.

It was not until March 1987 that a major change was made to the Lagonda with the launch of the Series 4 at the Geneva Motor Show (where Zagato showed its hideous Lagonda

Rapide, which fortunately never saw the production light of day). Replacing the touch buttons were more practical push-buttons and gone were the waistline rubbing strips and the pop-up headlamps, the latter replaced by what appeared to be a six-gun battery in the nose, while the generally sharp-edged lines were smoothed out and a deep chin spoiler, complete with foglamps, and side skirts were added, while the fuel fillers were moved from the C-pillars to the bottom of the rear screen, as on the Aston V8. Indeed, not one of the aluminium panels remained the same as the Series 2 and 3

cars, although the altered dimensions retained the original length of 17ft 4in and width of 5ft 11½in. Accordingly, the price rose to no less than £85,000. As with the Series 5 Aston V8, power was now quoted, and for the first time it equalled that of the Aston at 305bhp at 5,500rpm with 340lb/ft of torque at 4,000rpm. Wheels were also changed from steel to light alloy, with the diameter increased to 16in, but still 7in wide and with lower-profile 255/60 VR16 CR27 Avon Turbospeeds. While weight had increased over the Series 2 and 3 models, so had power, and performance remained

The 1984 long-wheelbase limited edition by Tickford. At a cost of £110,000 only three examples were ever sold.

For the Series 4 version of the V8 Lagonda, Towns' sharp lines were rounded-off, giving the car a generally chunkier appearance.

much the same. In May 1988 *Fast Lane* magazine recorded the 0 to 60mph sprint in 8.4 seconds (midway between the October 1980 *Motor* and *Autocar* figures), 0 to 100mph in 20.7 seconds and a top speed of 145mph. Production of the Series 4 Lagonda (at the rate of one per week) ceased in January 1990 with chassis number LOJR 13645, but it is planned to launch a successor to this unique sporting and luxury four-door carriage at the 1991 German Motor Show.

CHAPTER 6

V8 engine in competition – 1

Return to Le Mans and national racing

Aston Martins have a very solid tradition of racing and after the launch of the DBS V8 it was not long before the model first appeared in competition, Aston Martin Owners Club member Peter Foden putting himself in the record book in 1970 when he took third place in one of the club's sprints at Curborough in a standard car. He was alone, however, in entering his DBS V8 in such events until Aston dealer Robin Hamilton competed at Curborough in 1974.

Derbyshire-based Hamilton had begun part-time dealing in cars while serving an apprenticeship at Rolls-Royce, and his first experience of Astons was with a DB5. Soon after, realizing the potential for a specialized Aston service in the Midlands, he set up Robin Hamilton Motors in Tutbury with engineer David Jack. It then occurred to him that competition exposure with an Aston would be beneficial to his business and he duly purchased a DB4 GT. That well and truly set the ball rolling, Hamilton going on to become an innovative and prominent figure in Aston Martin competition circles.

In 1973 Robin Hamilton Motors was appointed an official Aston Martin Service Agent and the following April Hamilton entered chassis DBSV8/10038/RC at Curborough, the same car that in highly modified form three years later was to take Aston Martin back to Le Mans for the first time since 1964. In the interim, DBSV8/10038/RC was gradually developed, first into a Group 5 car with an AM V8 single-headlight front end to keep the Aston's identity in line with current models. Already the aim was long-distance racing, and the factory assisted in homologating the car for

international competition with both the FIA and the RAC Motor Sports Association.

In Group 5 trim, power from the 5.3-litre V8 was estimated at something over 400bhp courtesy of modified cylinder heads, higher-lift camshafts, quadruple sidedraught Weber carburettors and a special exhaust system. Despite the comparatively modest power output, the DBS V8, with racing tyres, lowered suspension and uprated brakes, performed well in club racing events, power then being further increased with four downdraught Weber carburettors. The car had also benefited from a free two-week run on Aston's own engine test-bed overseen by engine man Dave Morgan, and a factory-funded wind-tunnel session at MIRA which resulted in the adoption of a rear boot spoiler and front air dam, looking not dissimilar to those of the V8 Vantage model that was to appear in 1977.

Hamilton had originally planned to enter the 1976 Le Mans 24 Hours race, but finance was lacking and many were dubious that his dream of taking Aston back to the Sarthe circuit would materialize. But even the factory's managing director of the time, Fred Hartley, promised some sponsorship, though with the financial crisis at Newport Pagnell at this time it was not surprising that the promise could not be fulfilled.

By the winter of 1976 some sponsorship had been found from SAS, a security and anti-riot equipment company, while the DBS V8 by this time was so highly modified that Hamilton changed the chassis number to RHAM 1. The V8 engine now featured forged Cosworth pistons and Nimonic

The 520bhp engine of the Hamilton Le Mans DBS V8.

valves and with quadruple 50 IDA downdraught Webers power was quoted as 520bhp at 6,750rpm, with in excess of 400lb/ft of torque. A large tail spoiler was fitted to reduce dangerously high lift at speed, and to improve the weight bias the radiator was moved to the rear of the car which, following further wind-tunnel tests, it was estimated would improve top speed by 10mph through reduced drag. However, insufficient engine cooling resulted, so the radiator had to be returned to the front of the car while four oil coolers ensured that the oil would stay within its temperature limits. The chassis had also been extensively modified, notably with a redesigned front bulkhead, a very substantial roll-cage was fitted, while specially made centre-lock, 19in diameter magnesium wheels, 15in wide at the rear, 13in at the front, were fitted with Dunlop tyres. Stopping them were massive 12½in ventilated, twin-caliper Lockheed disc brakes all round, something of a necessity with an all-up weight of

Robin Hamilton's very modified DBS V8, alias RHAM 1, prior to Le Mans in 1977, where it finished a commendable 17th.

A month earlier it made its race debut in the Silverstone 6 Hours. Robin Hamilton, with sunglasses, is peering over the engine.

For 1979, RHAM 1 was turbocharged and the body substantially modified. At Le Mans, however, the racer retired after just 2¾ hours.

30cwt and an estimated top speed of 190mph.

RHAM 1 made its debut at the Silverstone Six Hours in May 1977, traditionally the warm-up to Le Mans, Hamilton being co-driven by fellow AMOC member and dentist Dave Preece. After a minor practice 'off', the big Aston qualified on the eighth row of the grid with a time of 1 minute 43.39 seconds and ran well until excessive heat from the inboard rear discs led to failure of the differential oil seals. Much time was lost, but the car finished, albeit without qualifying, too few laps having been covered. The potential, however, was there and Silverstone provided the opportunity to sort out previously unknown gremlins, a differential oil cooler, for example, subsequently being fitted.

At Le Mans, veteran Mike Salmon – who had driven the last Aston to race at Le Mans in 1964, Project 214 – was drafted in as the third driver, while some additional sponsorship had been raised through the AMOC, subscribing members having their names written on the Aston's rear valance. In wet conditions on the first day the car, running in the GTP class, qualified in mid-field of the 60-car grid with a top speed of 188mph recorded along the Mulsanne Straight, but in the next day's dry session RHAM 1, which incidentally was giving away 5½cwt to the next heaviest car, was pushed right down the order. When the organizers reduced the number of starters to 55 the Aston's best lap of 4 minutes 31.8 seconds was not good enough for inclusion, but fortunately another runner was found to have illegal modifications and its removal allowed the Aston to run after all.

In the race, the Aston thundered around, picking up 23 places in the first two hours until cracked brake discs, estimated to be running as hot as 700°C, necessitated a lengthy stop. Thereafter, the brakes were used as little as possible, but otherwise the car ran reliably, Robin Hamilton himself taking the car across the line 17th overall and third in the GTP class. It was a superb effort and mud in the eye of those who had doubted the team's ability to fulfil the Le Mans dream.

It had been planned to compete again in the 1978 Le Mans race, but insufficient finances decreed otherwise, then in 1979 a package was put together for RHAM 1, with a notable contribution from another AMOC member, Peter Millward (subsequently the owner of one of the Lola-Aston Martins). By now the Aston was sporting a pair of Garrett AiResearch turbochargers and lower-compression Cosworth pistons. Thus equipped, 600bhp was available at just 4,000rpm, rising to a peak of around 800bhp at 6,000rpm with prodigious torque! However, as we have seen in the previous chapter, although Aston Martin was experimenting at the time with the twin-turbocharged Lagonda (while John Pope was the first to turbocharge the Aston V8), the factory was not involved. No-one at the time had a great deal of experience using forced induction on the Aston V8, and this and a lack of development time were to be reflected in RHAM 1's subsequent outings.

For 1978 RHAM 1 had been turbocharged, but for 1979 radical alterations were also made to the body, the roof line being cut down by 3in and the nose lowered in order to improve the car's aerodynamics. Excessive fuel consumption was overcome by substituting fuel injection for the carburettors, but there was no sign of an intercooler, which meant additional oil cooling had to be directed at the underside of the V8's pistons. The brakes also received additional cooling and around 350lb was knocked off the car's weight.

In this guise, though with the turbo boost turned down to give a mere 650bhp in the interests of reliability, RHAM 1 appeared at the Silverstone Six Hours, Hamilton and Preece this time being joined by World Sportscar Champion Derek Bell. In prior testing Bell had been surprised by the car's performance and his lap times in the wet had proved as quick as those achieved in the dry two years earlier. During practice for the Six Hours, Hamilton suffered a de Dion tube breakage (there were also to be hub and driveshaft failures) which was an unheard-of failure, probably caused by the V8's considerable torque which, in this low-boost form, still yielded 600lb/ft. Fortunately, an accident was avoided and the car was able to be repaired.

For the race Hamilton opted to concentrate on the pit work, leaving Bell and Preece to share the driving after Bell had put the Aston 11th on the 25-car grid with a best time of 1min 37.54sec. All appeared to be going well until the brakes began to fade rapidly while the oil catch tank started to fill at an alarming rate. The latter problem was caused by the oil system over-scavenging and regular half-hour halts became necessary to drain the system. At one stage the car had dropped to 21st position, though at the flag the Aston crossed the line in 13th place. Bell reported that it had been the only car that could gain on the Porsche 935s down the straights.

For the 1979 Le Mans race, RHAM 1 featured a water-injection cooling system and additional ducting for the hard-pressed brakes, but all the extra equipment required helped to increase weight to 30kg above the 1977 figure. Hamilton and Preece were again joined by Salmon, who put in the best lap of 4min 24.48sec, over 7½ seconds faster than two years earlier. The aerodynamics, however, were less effective and top speed on the Mulsanne Straight was little different. In the race, with less than an hour run, RHAM 1 had to be pitted with a mystery oil leak and excessive water temperature. Unfortunately, the situation was not to improve and after 2¾ hours a broken con-rod ended the Aston's run as Salmon set

The home-built Gipfast Special of Dave Preece shortly after completion in early 1980.

Sadly, the Gipfast Special's only race was the Silverstone 6 Hours, where it retired early on with suspension failure

off on his first lap. Later it was also discovered that a piston had melted, the resultant hole allowing oil to pass through under high revs and increase crankcase pressure, ultimately breaking the crankshaft oil seal, hence the mystery leak – at idle in the pits it had not been evident.

As far as Robin Hamilton was concerned, that was the end of the road for his heavily modified DBS V8, and all efforts were then turned to an exciting Aston-engined Group C project, although RHAM 1 did take part in the 1980 Six Hours, Bell sharing with Hamilton, but its retirement after 61 miles through engine failure was a sad end to a brave effort. Robin, though, ever one to make good use of publicity, later used the car to set a new world land speed record for towing a caravan at Elvington Airfield on October 14, 1980. With the turbocharger boost turned up to 18psi to achieve the full 800bhp, and in pouring rain, RHAM 1 managed to record 152mph towing a 15cwt Alpha caravan, with a mean speed of 125mph, comfortably beating the previous record of 108mph – apparently more than a little care was needed to stop the combination on the relatively short runway!

While Hamilton concentrated on getting the Group C project together, Dave Preece had already begun work on his own mid-engined machine. He had been against turbocharging the Aston V8, believing a normally aspirated unit would be better employed in a purpose-built machine which, through being lighter, would make life easier for the brakes. Together with motor engineer Ken Heywood, Preece set about designing and building a proper race car for the 1980 Le Mans, work starting in his underground garage in late 1979.

Bearing the chassis number DP/801/H, a central tub was formed as a sheet aluminium spaceframe with body panels riveted in place. It had been decided to run the car in the GT Prototype class and as such a spare wheel had to be carried while a rear window and provision for luggage space had to be included in the design, these requirements, combined with 19in diameter wheels to aid top speed, accounting for the rather bulbous shape. Suspension centred around Lola magnesium uprights with rocker arms, inboard dampers and coil springs at the front and reversed bottom wishbones at the

Hyde Vale's heavily modified DBS V8 is harried by Dave Ellis' mighty V8. (Behind is one of the RS Williams lightweight DB4 racers.)

rear. Brakes were large 12.4in and 12in ventilated discs at front and rear, respectively, in keeping with the estimated top speed of 200mph provided by a 480bhp (at 7,000rpm) engine built by AVJ Engineering in Pershore. The V8 was mated to a Hewland LG600 transaxle via a four-plate clutch (RHAM 1 had used a triple-plate clutch).

After a variety of last-minute hitches, the car, now known as the Gipfast Special, sponsorship having been acquired from the paint manufacturer, appeared for its debut at the Silverstone Six Hours, Simon Phillips and Richard Jenvey sharing the driving with Preece. It had been completed just 10 hours before, and it was a blow when the engine started to seize after only 10 laps of practice, the cause being a spacer between engine and transaxle being fractionally too long and putting too much pressure on the crankshaft thrust washers. Aston Martin, however, was swift to offer the factory facilities and by early the following day the car was running again, only to break a driveshaft. The Gipfast made the start in 30th spot, however, but sadly, after so much effort, its race was soon over when a rear suspension balljoint sheared, the car retiring on the spot. The Six Hours was to be the only time the Gipfast raced, the car being withdrawn from the impending Le Mans race after testing revealed a dangerous tendency to weave under braking from high speed. There was insufficient time to make the necessary suspension alterations and, having failed to generate any home sponsorship, DP/801/H was cut up and disposed of.

Preece, however, was undeterred and, still believing the Aston V8 engine to be ideal for endurance racing, he commissioned William Towns to design a suitable body. This got as far as a quarter-scale wind-tunnel model which revealed a 0.29 Cd and looked not dissimilar to the Bulldog prototype. The chassis and suspension were computer-designed (CAD) and the estimated top speed was 225mph. Once again, though, insufficient funds were available and the project was scrapped.

Despite these setbacks, Preece and Heywood did build one more car, this time one that actually resembled an Aston Martin. Using glassfibre front and rear body panels bought from Robin Hamilton, Heywood constructed another aluminium spaceframe tub resembling a production V8, but with some ground effect built in at the rear. Carrying chassis number DP/812/H, the racer looked like a cross between a V8 Vantage and RHAM 1 in 1977 guise. The 480bhp engine was retained and the Hewland transmission replaced by a conventional five-speed ZF gearbox and rear axle. The main aim, under the new fuel-conscious Group C regulations of the World Endurance Championship, was still Le Mans, although the car could also be used for AMOC and other club racing events, hence the standard production uprights of the front suspension in contrast to the Lola uprights and outboard coil springs of the rear suspension.

With a weight of around 1,100kg, some 750kg lighter than a standard Aston V8, and with 480bhp, an impressive performance was anticipated when DP/812/H made its debut at the Brands Hatch 1,000kms race in October 1982, Reg Woodcock co-driving. Unfortunately, Preece's luck was not to change and he aquaplaned off in appallingly wet conditions on the first lap, immobilizing the car with a bent wheel rim, but only slightly damaging the bodywork. However, the story was very different at a subsequent Intermarque race between club teams of Astons, Jaguars, ACs and Porsches, when the car, despite starting from the back of the grid and spinning twice, won the race! It was later banned from these club races and, finally calling it a day, Preece sold his last Aston-engined race car in 1982.

Two other heavily modified V8 Aston Martins were contesting AMOC club races around this time and are worthy of mention. The first, and the most successful racing Aston Martin ever, was the yellow V8 Saloon of Wigan-based plant hire company owner Dave Ellis. After a win at a Curborough sprint in another Aston in 1977, Ellis decided to try his hand at circuit racing and with his AM V8, chassis number V8/10610/RCA, he set out to beat Jaguar, Porsche and Ferrari. Gradually, the Aston, which has since been completely modified and maintained in-house by Ellis, became more and more rapid, notching up wins wherever it appeared. However, in 1982 it was decided to drastically modify the Aston and around half the original chassis was removed and replaced with steel box-sections while the body itself was lightened and lowered between 3 and 4 inches on the chassis. The engine and gearbox were then moved back in the chassis by a foot and 12in ventilated disc brakes were

The 540bhp engine of Hyde Vale's 'Silver Dream Racer'.

fitted all round to help stop the 500bhp machine that now weighed just 22cwt. So equipped, Ellis continued to win virtually all the races he entered, the car proving able to lap Silverstone faster than a Lola T70. By 1986 the engine and gearbox had been moved back another foot, while the power of the homebuilt Aston V8 engine, still retaining its 5.3-litre capacity, had increased to an estimated 600bhp! It was little surprise that Dave Ellis and the yellow Aston won 30 of the 35 races entered in 1986, and eight of the 10 races entered in both 1988 and 1989, including one in which the car lapped a Ford GT40 at Brands Hatch! Plans were afoot to further modify this incredible Aston for the 1990 season.

A regular opponent of the Ellis V8 was the heavily modified DBS V8 of Aston agent Hyde Vale Garage, also known as the Silver Dream Racer, and driven by Hyde Vale director Ray Taft. This car, chassis number DBSV8/10330/RCA, had begun its racing life in 1979 in relatively standard form, though subsequent development was a little less radical than that of the Ellis car. The car missed the 1981 season, but when it reappeared in 1982 the chassis forward of the front crossmember and aft of the rear axle had been replaced by tubular steel subframes. The engine was also moved back in the chassis, though only by 9 inches, and 12in ventilated disc brakes were fitted while the V8 engine now produced 500bhp according to Aston's own dynamometer. This combination was enough to yield seven wins and six second places out of 15 races in 1982. The following season the engine was moved back again to a total distance of 17½in and placed 5in lower in the chassis than standard, and a lightweight windscreen was fitted in the quest to reduce overall weight, which came down to just over 24cwt. It was in this guise that the Hyde Vale car proved a match for the Ellis V8, the duo on occasion running neck-and-neck. Subsequent modifications included a power increase to an estimated 540bhp and in 1983 Ray Taft won the ASCAR Championship, a feat repeated by Ellis in 1984. After the 1983 season, Hyde Vale retired from racing, but the Silver Dream Racer appeared again in 1989 having been prepared by new owner Marsh Plant Hire. With Gerry Marshall driving it won all six Intermarque races entered and, like the Ellis car, was due to race again in 1990.

The Ellis V8 about to pass the less radically modified V8 of Mike Cousins at the 1989 AMOC Oulton Park meeting.

The performance of these two very rapid Astons later led road haulier Mike Cousins to build his own V8 for the 1984 season. Sporting a 490bhp engine a foot back in the chassis, this also proved successful, taking an ASCAR Championship and winning several Intermarque events.

Mention must be made again of John Pope's amazing Aston Martin-Vauxhall Magnum, which ultimately featured twin turbocharging. Farmer Pope, another AMOC member,

created this car in 1973 using a crashed DBS V8 and a Vauxhall Magnum bodyshell, the intention being to contest Super Saloon events where virtually any configuration was allowed. The Magnum shell was the only Vauxhall part used and Pope simply mated this to the Aston Martin's engine, gearbox, rear axle and suspensions by lowering the shell onto these components on his garage floor. Surprisingly little cutting, mostly to the car's front and rear bulkheads, was

Dave Ellis' phenomenal V8 in its late-1989 guise with 600bhp in just 22 hundredweight!

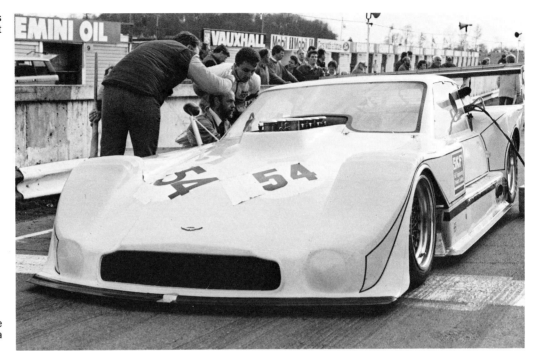

Boasting a mere 490bhp, the Cousins V8 racer was nonetheless a very effective machine.

needed to adapt the Aston running gear.

Carrying its own chassis number FJP/0001, this Aston/Vauxhall hybrid first ran in standard DBS V8 tune while the suspension was suitably stiffened and hefty anti-roll bars fitted with 15in x 12in wheels at the front, 15in x 15in at the rear. In its first race it finished sixth, and thereafter never finished lower than this during the 1974 season. As it was obviously not yet a winner, John Pope decided to fit twin turbochargers, having approached Dave Morgan at the Aston factory as to how most easily to increase power. The resulting conversion, the first time the Aston V8 engine was ever fitted with turbochargers, used two Garrett TO4 units and at first ran with a capacity of 5.2 litres due to a lack of suitably low-compression pistons. Soon after, the original 5.3-litre capacity was restored with 6.0:1 pistons and in this specification, after the Bosch injection had been carefully recalibrated, 600bhp at 6,000rpm was recorded with a very impressive 570lb/ft of torque. The subsequent fitment of twin intercoolers saw the respective output figures rise to 700bhp at 6,000rpm and a massive 700lb/ft of torque at 5,000rpm!

Not surprisingly, this turbocharged hybrid was endowed with phenomenal acceleration, and watercooled AP Racing discs with four-pot calipers were fitted to prevent cracking and ensure that the car stopped. Further modifications were carried out on the V8 which, now running 16½psi as opposed to 18psi boost, with the injection further altered and with 7.5:1 pistons, then produced a mind-blowing 820bhp at 6,250rpm combined with an incredible 760lb/ft of torque at 5,500rpm! Naturally, with this sort of power, underbonnet temperatures were always going to be high, but reliability was reasonable and the saloon car provided an unusual sight when overtaking some very fast purpose-built sports-racers. Although John Pope often raced the car himself, with moderate success, others also had a go, amongst them Ray Mallock and Gerry Marshall, the latter winning the car's last race, an Allcomers event, in 1982. This incredibly fast Aston/Vauxhall hybrid still exists and is occasionally given spirited outings on the road!

CHAPTER 7

V8 engine in competition – 2

Nimrod, EMKA and Cheetah-AMs

During the period between the 1979 Le Mans race and the construction of Dave Preece's 1982 Aston Martin Special, Hamilton's own Group C project had become considerably advanced. In late 1978 he had commissioned Lola's Eric Broadley (whose company had produced the famous GT40 as well as the Lola-Astons) to produce an up-to-the-minute chassis to take on Porsche in the WEC, particularly at Le Mans. Broadley thus produced the T385 tub using a wide, flat aluminium and dural monocoque with inboard rear suspension and a rear end which allowed the semi-stressed engine and mechanicals to be detached in minutes. Massive 13.4in Lockheed discs with four-pot calipers were fitted all round and either 16in or 19in diameter wheels were used.

Initially, Hamilton intended the sports-racer to be sold without engine so that customers could fit whatever powertrain they desired, but then he struck up a deal with Victor Gauntlett, whose Pace Petroleum company had recently acquired a 50% stake in Aston Martin Lagonda. Together with Peter Livanos, they formed Nimrod Racing Automobiles in September 1981, the name Nimrod meaning 'mighty long distance hunter'. All three shareholders were of like mind in wanting to see Aston Martin return to Le Mans once more, and if it was not feasible to build an Aston Martin for the job, then the next best thing was a car using a racing version of Aston Martin's trusty V8. NRA would in effect be a semi-works team and Gauntlett accordingly stipulated that the engine must be prepared by Aston Martin Tickford, and any racing feedback had to be made available for the benefit of the production cars – the basic reason, after all, why any manufacturer goes motor racing.

At this stage it was believed that the Group C regulations would be compatible with those for the American IMSA series. However, as so often seems to be the case with FISA, hopes of stability went out of the window; not only was the minimum weight reduced from 1,000 to 800kg and the use of some ground effects allowed, effectively making the flat-bottomed Nimrod an outdated leviathan from the start, but agreement could not be reached between FISA and IMSA. Consequently, Peter Livanos withdrew from NRA in January 1982, causing an immediate cash shortfall which Gauntlett and Hamilton had to replace.

The prototype Nimrod-Aston Martin, chassis NRAC1/001 (at race meetings it was always referred to as an Aston Martin-Nimrod, FISA requiring the engine manufacturer's name to come first, confusing some people into believing the car to be an Aston Martin), was initially tested by Derek Bell at Silverstone, then demonstrated by both Stirling Moss and James Hunt at Goodwood on November 19, 1981. The C1 part of the chassis number, incidentally, denoted an IMSA chassis, which was heavier by some 50lb, and C2 a Group C machine.

Both the NRA works Nimrod-Aston, chassis number NRAC2/003, and the privately-entered car, chassis NRAC2/004, of AMOC president Viscount Downe made their race debuts at the Silverstone 1,000kms in May 1982, this event replacing the old Six Hours. Lord Downe had been impressed by the Nimrod at its public showing at the Dubai Grand Prix during December 1981, while Pace Petroleum was happy to underwrite some of the costs, effectively making

Nimrod-Aston Martin line-up before the 1982 Silverstone 1,000Kms. On the left is the works NRA car, in the middle the private entry of AMOC president Lord Downe, and on the right the prototype.

a two-car team. The Downe car, however, was prepared and maintained entirely separately from the NRA car by Aston specialist (and manager of the 1989 Aston works team) Richard Williams, who virtually rebuilt the car once in his south-east London workshops, including considerable suspension changes suggested by driver and engineer Ray Mallock. Both cars used the Tickford-built engines, but after the Hamilton car suffered several failures in testing, Williams decided to play safe and use a rev limit of 6,500rpm, well below Tickford's recommended 7,250rpm limit at which the V8 was claimed to produce 580bhp.

At Silverstone, the works Nimrod, driven by Tiff Needell, Geoff Lees and Bob Evans, qualified on the seventh row with

1min 25.33sec, while the Downe car, with Mike Salmon sharing with Mallock, qualified one row ahead with 1min 24.88sec. Even so, it was some way off the equally new (and soon to be all-conquering) Porsche 956, which took pole position with a time almost 8 seconds quicker. At first both Nimrods ran well, their thunderous V8s sounding superb, but then the works car retired with engine problems, having already dropped a valve during practice. The Downe car, despite heavy oil consumption, otherwise proved totally reliable and the Nimrod 004 crossed the line sixth overall and fourth in Group C, an encouraging result on the car's debut.

Prior to Le Mans, engine troubles continued to plague the works Nimrod while the Downe car benefited from further

70

Both the works and Downe Nimrod-Astons debuted at Silverstone in 1982. Here, the private entry, which went on to finish sixth, makes a pit stop. The NRA car retired with engine problems.

The works Nimrod was also to retire at Le Mans after crashing, but the Downe/Williams car crossed the line in seventh place after losing compression. Note the traditional Aston-shaped radiator intake.

suspension changes by Ray Mallock. For the 24-hour classic, Williams set a rev limit of 6,250rpm, although Tickford was now recommending 7,000rpm, the Downe car's limit costing up to 40bhp. Driver teams were as at Silverstone except that Mallock and Salmon were joined by Simon Phillips.

Scrutineering proved typically awkward and the windscreen height of both Nimrods was found to be too low, Hamilton curing the problem by raising the ride height and Williams by fitting an extension resembling a taxi's roof light to the top of the screen, rather than upsetting suspension settings. As at Silverstone, the Downe car, which for Le Mans had substantial backing from Pace Petroleum, was the lighter of the two at 1,047kg against 1,051kg, but both were considerably overweight. Nonetheless, the cars were by no means slow, recording between 200 and 210mph along Mulsanne, but there was a problem with the rear Avon tyres separating from the wheel rims at such high speed. Mallock duly set the fastest time for the Downe car with a very respectable 3min 46.34sec with Needell not far behind on 3min 48.17sec, but again both well down on the 3min 28.4sec of the pole-sitting works Porsche 956. The normally aspirated Nimrod-Astons, of course, would be able to run close to these practice times in the race, whereas the drivers of the turbocharged cars, having turned up the wick for qualifying, would have to reduce the boost considerably during the race to avoid running out of fuel.

Both Nimrods ran strongly during the early stages of the race, the works car ahead with its higher rev limit. Then, after a little more than three and a half hours, with Needell in seventh position and Mallock running ninth, the works Nimrod crashed heavily on Mulsanne at around 200mph after a rear tyre deflated. After a ferocious spin, during which the car ricocheted between the heavy Armco barriers, Needell climbed out unscathed. Happily, although the car was badly damaged at the rear, the cockpit was still intact, an indication of the strength of modern racing machines.

While the crash was a bitter blow, the private Nimrod continued to circulate well with good fuel economy and by 2am it had climbed to fifth place and was the leading non-turbocharged car. Two hours later it was not only in fourth place but threatening the third-placed Porsche 936, a

position it held until late on Sunday morning. Then, with under five and a half hours remaining, trouble struck, a burnt-out exhaust valve reducing the Aston V8 to seven cylinders. Mallock and Salmon nursed the car round the circuit, dropping to eighth place, until Mallock became stranded on Mulsanne with no fuel pressure. Eventually, he got the engine restarted and after further time in the pits, Nimrod 004 rejoined the fray, but it was to become slower and slower as the compression wilted. Eventually, after a final lap which took an agonizing 7 minutes, it crossed the line in seventh place, a Porsche 936 and a Ferrari Boxer ahead having retired. It was an immensely popular result, not least for the huge British contingent present, and a worthy achievement for an underfinanced, private team which provided a great fillip for everyone concerned with the Nimrod-Aston project. Afterwards, an engine check revealed compression on just five cylinders.

Sadly for Robin Hamilton and NRA, however, Lady Luck was not one of their allies. Engine problems persisted, the team experiencing 15 failures, yet in contrast the Downe car had used just one engine all along, albeit with a lower rev limit. At the next round of the WEC, the Spa 1,000kms at Spa Francorchamps in Belgium – which the Downe car only made at the 11th hour, so short was finance – Mallock qualified the private machine 13th and Lees the NRA car in 18th place. Both Nimrods had their share of minor problems, climbing, dropping and then climbing again through the field. Sadly, the works car's growing engine misfires culminated in another failure, but the Downe car crossed the line in 11th spot, seventh in Group C and good enough to climb into third place in the championship behind Porsche and Rondeau. It was an incredible result considering the limited budget and the fact that just three races had been contested!

While the result was also satisfying for the enthusiastic Robin Hamilton, the instigator of the whole Nimrod-Aston Martin project, he decided to call it a day in Europe and take his équipe to America to contest IMSA events, no money being left after Pace withdrew its backing. Links were duly severed with Victor Gauntlett and Tickford, the latter much to Hamilton's relief, and chassis 003 was shipped out together with a new IMSA-specification chassis, NRAC1/002.

Prior to leaving for America, the works Nimrod-Aston made one more UK appearance when, as a publicity stunt, it was pitched against a No 42 Squadron Nimrod reconnaissance aircraft at RAF St Mawgan in Cornwall. On a wet November 28, 1982, with Bob Evans driving the Group C car and Flt Lt Steve Smith piloting the aircraft, the two machines were timed over the standing kilometre. Despite the 11,500lb/ft of thrust generated by the plane's quadruple Rolls-Royce Spey jet engines, it could not match the Nimrod-Aston's acceleration, the best times over two runs being 21.8 and 22.6sec for the car and 25.6 and 23.0sec for the aircraft, with a terminal speed of 180mph!

The Downe car in the meantime went on to contest the Brands Hatch 1,000kms race on October 17, the last round of the WEC, but counting only for the drivers' championship. To increase front-end downforce a full-width wing ran across the nose of the Nimrod, which also sported new-found sponsorship from the construction group Bovis. On a wet track Mallock, again sharing with Salmon, qualified 12th fastest and in a race where track conditions were appalling due to heavy rain (with many cars skidding off, the Preece V8 Special amongst them) the duo brought the car home ninth out of 21 finishers from the 35-car grid.

Over the ensuing winter, much development work was carried out on Nimrod 004 by Ray Mallock and Richard Williams, including a new lighter and far more slippery body shape with greater downforce, while backing for the full season had been obtained from Bovis. Meanwhile, in America, Hamilton was to contest the NRA team's first IMSA event, the famous Daytona 24 Hours, in early February 1983 and he achieved quite a coup by securing not only hefty backing from race sponsor Pepsi-Cola, but also the services of American legend A.J. Foyt. Sharing with him in chassis 002 – renamed the Pepsi Challenger for the event – were NASCAR champion Darrel Waltrip, Tiff Needell and Argentine F2 champion Guillermo Maldonado, with chassis 003, as always in its green and silver NRA livery, piloted by Drake Olsen, Lyn St James and Canadian ex-skater John Graham.

Nimrod 003 qualified 12th at 1min 49.39sec, one place ahead of the lighter IMSA car on 1min 50.00sec, and they

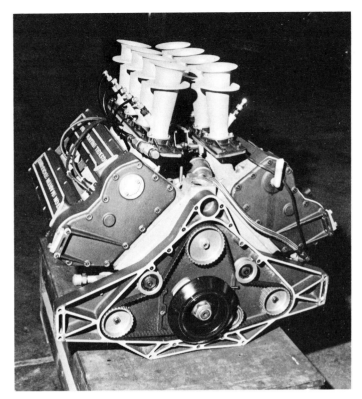

Aston Martin Tickford produced this shortened and lightened version of the racing V8 engine for the EMKA-Aston Martin of 1983.

were the fastest non-turbo cars. The race was to be notable as the first confrontation at modern international level between Aston Martin and Jaguar, the Bob Tullius 570bhp Jaguar XJR5 making its debut at Daytona and qualifying between the two Nimrods with a time of 1min 49.82sec. It was to come to nothing, however, the Pepsi Challenger retiring after 121 laps with engine failure after the sump baffles had worked loose, the works car going the same way 81 laps later after nine hours of racing. The engines were the last Tickford units to be used by NRA, and from then on Hamilton elected that the team would build its own engines.

The EMKA-Aston leads the Downe/Williams Nimrod-Aston through the Esses at Le Mans in 1983, the former going on to finish 17th.

A night pit stop for the sole Nimrod-Aston at Le Mans in 1983. It retired after 18 hours.

Finances were now rather depleted, and despite attracting some sponsorship, Hamilton was forced to offer rent-a-drives. At the team's next outing, the Miami Grand Prix in February, the rain was so heavy that the circuit became flooded and after just 27 laps the race was stopped. Doc Bundy and Lyn St James in 003, having qualified 16th, finished 20th, and Drake Olsen, this time sharing 002 with Victor Gonzales, crossed the line 16th, having qualified in 21st spot and at one stage having run in fourth place.

The resourceful Hamilton managed to enter both Nimrod-Astons in the Sebring 12 Hours in March, and the race was to give the marque its finest result ever. With 002 again driven by Olsen and Gonzales and St James joined by Reggie Smith in 002, the cars qualified 13th and a poor 48th, respectively, in a widely varied field that included the Tullius, Adam and Baird Jaguar XJR5, which qualified second fastest, and ageing saloon cars. In the race the IMSA Nimrod retired with a bent valve, followed soon after by the Jaguar, but the green and silver works car pulled steadily through the field to clinch fifth place overall. It was a fine result and one that

Robin Hamilton had well and truly earned.

Road Atlanta in April was the next venue for the IMSA/Camel GT series and this time Olsen was paired with St James in the Group C car that appeared without any sponsorship. The car qualified a respectable seventh fastest, but St James crashed in the race. Finances by now had well and truly deteriorated, so much so that Hamilton sold chassis 002 to Jack Miller. Consequently, only the old faithful works car ran at Riverside later that April and, after qualifying 12th, it was to retire after running over debris from the crashed Jaguar! Nonetheless, the spectators and the teams had enjoyed the sight of the Nimrod-Aston and the Jaguar running neck-and-neck for nearly an hour.

Through lack of cash, the works Nimrod was to miss the Lime Rock 3 Hours in May and Drake Olsen joined Jack Miller in 002. Not only did Olsen qualify the Nimrod ninth fastest and run as high as third place, but the car lapped the Jaguar XJR5 before retiring with transaxle failure. It was another encouraging performance and Hamilton put a deal together for the Mid-Ohio 6 Hours on June 19, facing the reality that Le Mans that year was an impossibility. Saloon racer Robert Overby rented a drive alongside Olsen in the works car, with Miller entering 002 for Carlos Ramirez and himself. The cars qualified 10th and 17th, respectively, but Overby was to crash out of the race while the IMSA car finished a lowly 28th.

By now Nimrod Racing Automobiles' coffers were less than bare and on August 22, 1983 the company was wound up, Robin Hamilton being forced to liquidate his Aston dealership as well to cover the substantial debts that had accrued. However, he had proved that the Nimrod-Aston Martins had the potential to run competitively. Jack Miller continued to campaign chassis 002, regularly sharing driving duties with Carlos Ramirez, their results including retirement at Pocono in September, having qualified 13th, and eighth overall at the Daytona 3 Hours in November, having qualified 24th. Joined by Vicky Smith, this trio were to retire at the Daytona 24 Hours in early February, 1984, followed by another retirement in the Miami Grand Prix, Ramirez crashing after Miller had qualified 25th fastest. Yet another retirement ensued at Watkins Glen, though at the Lime Rock

2 Hours in February, 1985 Miller finished in 10th place, after qualifying 13th, and followed this with two more finishes later that year, taking 16th place in the Mid-Ohio 3 Hours and 15th in the Columbus 4 Hours.

Although Nimrod Racing Automobiles was no more, it must be mentioned that an evolution Nimrod, the C3, had been part of the major plan from the start, but sadly it was never to come to fruition. Its history dates back to late 1981 and, constructed in carbon-fibre and Kevlar honeycomb, it was advanced for the time, using a basically triangular tub shape for maximum strength. Five Nimrods in either IMSA (C1) or Group C (C2) form were completed, and the one tub produced thus bore the chassis number NRAC3/006. It also made full use of ground effect aerodynamics with the plan to use light-alloy castings extensively throughout the car's construction. Interestingly, a normally aspirated 6-litre

At the Silverstone 1,000Kms in 1984 one Nimrod-Aston ran with twin turbochargers. It proved disastrous and was retired after 40 laps. Note the side exhausts.

version of Aston Martin's V8 was to be employed and, still using two valves per cylinder, 650bhp was hoped for. Such a package could well have had great potential but the liquidation of Nimrod Racing Automobiles meant that it would never be realized.

At one stage, Viscount Downe and Victor Gauntlett considered purchasing the Nimrod C3 project, but overall financial considerations precluded this. The team was thus to continue with its own evolution Nimrod, which was said to produce double the downforce of the original body shape with weight considerably reduced to 940kg. Contributing to this was a Tickford engine with lighter liners and pistons accounting for a 20lb saving.

Another Aston V8-engined car to join the WEC fray in 1983 was the EMKA-Aston Martin of Steve O'Rourke run by Michael Cane Racing. AMOC member O'Rourke, manager of the pop group Pink Floyd, had raced at Le Mans in 1982 with the group's drummer Nick Mason in a Group 5 BMW M1. When O'Rourke wanted to build a Group C car he contacted Michael Cane, who reasoned that a car weighing 850 kilos, the new minimum weight (as opposed to 800), with some ground effect aerodynamics and the proven Tickford-Aston powerplant would be a competitive proposition. In order to keep the weight down Tickford was approached to convert the Aston V8 engine to a fully stressed member and reposition some of the ancilliaries, such as replacing the water pump with twin pumps either side of the engine, to assist underbody aerodynamics. Such changes, together with a new end plate to allow the V8 to be mounted as a fully stressed member, resulted in a new block casting with a length reduced by $4\frac{1}{2}$in, a height reduced by $1\frac{1}{2}$in and a total weight saving of 50lb, while both the distributor and alternator were repositioned in the engine's V and a 10in flywheel replaced the normal 13in item. Tickford had already been working on improving the V8's characteristics, although plans to go the four-valve route were postponed until 1984 on the grounds of cost and time, and the power output was now quoted as 570bhp at 7,000rpm with maximum torque of 460lb/ft at 5,000rpm. Richard Williams, however, because the 'new' V8 was an untried engine, opted to have only the lighter pistons and liners, though the V8s supplied to Nimrod produced the same power figures.

The design of the EMKA was by Len Bailey, who had been responsible for the Ford GT40 and C100 sportscars amongst others. He produced an aluminium central monocoque with a flat bottom and twin underbody air tunnels with the Aston V8 bolted directly to the tub's rear. Front suspension was by the usual magnesium uprights with the coil spring/damper units fixed within the tub, while the rear suspension's wishbones and A-bracket were bolted directly to the Hewland transaxle, with rocker arms and coil spring/damper units fixed to the bellhousing, the idea being to prevent any suspension componentry impeding airflow. AP 12in disc brakes with four-pot calipers provided the stopping power.

The first appearance of the EMKA-Aston, chassis number C83/1, and the evolution Nimrod-Aston was at the Silverstone 1,000kms in May 1983. Mallock, as usual, co-drove with Salmon and qualified Nimrod 004 15th in 1min 22.70sec, the EMKA being close behind in 16th place with 1min 24.45sec by Tiff Needell, who was sharing with O'Rourke and saloon car ace Jeff Allam. In the race, the Nimrod soon rose to seventh place, which it held to the flag (bar a temporary drop when it struck a hare) while the EMKA, after various teething problems, was running ninth until a broken rear wing relegated it to 13th. Cruelly, a hub bearing failure on the final lap prevented the EMKA from finishing, but it had been a promising debut for both cars.

For Le Mans in 1983, Mallock and Salmon were joined by American Steve Earle, with Nick Faure and Tiff Needell teaming up with O'Rourke in the EMKA. The Nimrod proved heavier than anticipated, weighing 987kg in Le Mans trim, as did the EMKA at 900kg against the predicted 850kg. Prospects, however, looked very promising when Mallock qualified 12th fastest in the opening session and ultimately 16th fastest with a time of 3min 35.78sec, the Nimrod clocking 213mph on the Mulsanne Straight. The EMKA proved somewhat slower, recording 209mph, with Needell's best lap 3min 42.23sec, while Ickx in the pole-sitting Porsche 956 had recorded a sensational 3min 16.6sec lap on qualifying tyres and with high turbo boost.

Unfortunately, the Nimrod was plagued in the race, first with battery/electrical problems, then gear-selection difficulties, dropping it to 30th place at one point. It was to climb back up the field until, at 12.30am, Salmon was sprayed in the face with oil, the shock sending him into a spin; the problem had been caused by the troublesome electrics having burnt through an oil line. Repairs dropped the Nimrod to 31st, from which it rose again to 13th, but the time spent running with low oil (oil refills are regulated under the WEC rules) had taken its toll and the Nimrod retired in the 18th hour with a broken connecting rod.

The EMKA-Aston, meanwhile, had been delayed with a holed radiator, a damaged door and a cracked rear suspension wishbone, but thereafter it climbed steadily up the field from 29th to 19th before Nick Faure received a facefull of petrol! While the leak was being repaired it was discovered that both rear hub bearings needed replacement and further delays ensued to repair a door and the rear wing, but by the end of the 24 hours it was still running, crossing the line in 17th place and the first British car home, as the Nimrod-Aston had been the previous year.

The EMKA-Aston was not to make another appearance until 1985, but the Downe Nimrod was once more entered for the Spa 1,000kms in September, where Mallock qualified 14th with a best lap of 2min 23.92sec. After a steady run by both he and Salmon, the car was running seventh with an hour to go when a con-rod bolt failed. Things were to be no better at another wet Brands Hatch 1,000kms a fortnight later when, after qualifying 11th with a lap in 1min 25.16sec, the Nimrod retired with differential failure, having run as high as seventh. Nevertheless, the Nimrod-Aston Martin again took third place in the World Championship, this time behind Porsche and Lancia.

Reliability and fuel economy had been fortés of the Nimrod, and with the planned reduction from 100 to 85 litres maximum fuel for the 1984 season, it was felt that prospects were good if some more weight could be saved and a little more speed found. Bovis agreed to sponsor the Downe Nimrod, chassis 004, and NRAC2/005, which Victor Gauntlett had bought new in 1982 and sold, and Peter Livanos was about to acquire. Plans for 1984 were thus ambitious and included an entry at the Daytona 24 Hours

The 1984 Downe/AML Nimrod-Aston line-up. The smiles were not to last long.

over February 4/5, with additional funds coming from Peter Livanos/Aston Martin North America. Car 004 would run alongside 005, at this stage still owned by John Cooper (a privateer) and in original bodywork, with Bob Evans and Paul Smith co-driving. Mallock was joined by Drake Olsen and dentist John Sheldon and the two cars thus formed a team while, as already mentioned, Jack Miller entered 002 for himself, Carlos Ramirez and Vicky Smith.

Qualifying third fastest on the 82-car grid was the promising Group 44 Jaguar XJR5 of Tullius, Hobbs and Bundy, four places ahead of the Downe Nimrod, predictably the quickest of the trio. Mallock managed a best lap of 1min 56.82sec, 3 seconds behind the first XJR5 and only 4/10ths behind the second Jaguar of Brian Redman, Adam and Bedard, and aided by a special rear wing which increased downforce. Surprisingly, Nimrod 002 in 23rd spot was quicker than 005 in 26th, their respective times being 2min 5.39sec and 2min 5.68sec.

A tyre blow-out caused some steering damage and a delay for the Downe car in the race but, after further suspension problems and a blown head gasket, it managed to cross the line in 16th place. Nimrod 002 had retired just after half-distance with transmission failure, but 005 had a comfortable run and finished seventh. Soon after it was shipped to England, where it received similar evolution bodywork to 004, also benefiting from lighter Kevlar panels and titanium springs.

Before the Silverstone 1,000kms in May, FISA typically went back on the planned reduced fuel allowance which, together with a lack of sponsorship, was enough to cause the EMKA-Aston's withdrawal that season. Nimrod 005, in the meanwhile, had also been turbocharged to make use of the effectively increased allowance, using two Garrett TO4 turbos, 6psi boost and twin intercoolers from the experience gained with the similarly Garrett-equipped Lagonda and the Bulldog prototype. It was to be a big mistake, lacking in development and speed, the V8 when installed in this guise never being able to produce the 655bhp and 570lb/ft of torque in race trim recorded on Tickford's dynamometer (maxima of 710bhp and 710lb/ft had been seen), while Richard Williams was against forced induction from the start, the decision having been taken by Livanos and majority shareholder Papanicolaous.

During practice, 005's lack of power and development showed in Mallock's best qualifying time of 1min 23.59sec, putting it only one place ahead of 004 on 1min 24.48sec, the latter car being driven by Salmon, Sheldon and Richard Attwood. The turbocharged car, co-driven by Drake Olsen, was withdrawn just 40 laps into the race after far too lean a mixture had wrecked the liners, causing huge oil consumption and, to make matters worse, 004 also retired with a dropped valve.

For Le Mans, both Nimrods were normally aspirated and for the first time the Downe team had the luxury of one qualifying engine. The driver strength was as at Silverstone and also present (on the 25th anniversary of Aston Martin's victory at the Sarthe) were two Group 44 Jaguar XJR5s running in the GTP class. The works Porsche team, incidentally, had boycotted the event, having become fed up with FISA's lack of rule stability, though plenty of privateer Porsches were entered.

The single qualifying engine with increased rpm enabled Mallock to qualify 005 in 10th place with an impressive 3min 33.12sec, putting it four places ahead of the nearest Jaguar and making the Nimrod-Aston again the quickest non-turbo car. John Sheldon was fastest in the sister Nimrod, but could manage no better than 30th place with 3min 47.42sec. The battle that ensued between the leading Jaguar and Nimrod-Aston soon after the start was much appreciated by the huge British crowd and made a heart-warming sight, reminiscent of confrontations of old, with little to separate the two cars. Much place-swapping was to take place and at a little over the six-hour mark, 005 lay an impressive fifth, with 004 13th.

Disaster, however, was literally around the corner when John Sheldon crashed heavily on Mulsanne following a 200mph tyre blow-out. So severe was the impact that the car somersaulted the barriers and erupted in flames, a marshal being struck a fatal blow by an errant piece of suspension. The next car along was the Porsche 956 of Jonathan Palmer, who slammed on his brakes but, by a cruel stroke of luck, Drake Olsen, close behind Palmer, hit the barriers violently in trying to avoid the Porsche. Olsen was unhurt, but John Sheldon was severely burnt and it was to be some months

Engine change after practice, Le Mans 1984. The Tickford Aston V8 was claimed to produce around 575bhp.

before he was finally released from hospital. Thankfully, against initial predictions, not only is he still practising as a dentist, but also competing once more in sportscar events.

This double accident was bad enough in itself, but it was also a massive financial setback for the Downe team; 004 was all but written-off (it has since been rebuilt and is still owned by Lord Downe) while 005 was in a very sorry state (now also rebuilt and still owned by Livanos). Ironically, had 005 continued at the same pace at Le Mans it would have finished in third place. It was to be the end of Downe/Williams/AML team and a far cry from what could ultimately have been.

At the Spa 1,000kms in September, 1984 another Aston Martin V8-engined car was to pick up the Newport Pagnell mantle in the form of Swiss Chuck Graemiger's Cheetah G604. Notable as the first carbon-fibre composite monocoque on the Group C scene, the Cheetah-Aston Martin had been designed by engineer Graemiger himself with ground effect tunnels, its Kevlar chassis being built by Advanced Composites in Derby. Its Aston engine was the same as that in the EMKA – though the Cheetah was far lighter – while the front suspension used conventional

Nimrod-Aston Martin leads Jaguar XJR5 at the 1984 Le Mans. Soon after both Nimrods were eliminated in an horrific crash.

magnesium uprights and wishbone/coil springs and the rear had inboard coil spring/damper units. Backed by Gatoil, the car had been due to appear early in 1984, but various legal problems had precluded this.

Tickford was now claiming 580bhp for its Aston V8 and, combined with the 870kg weight recorded at Spa, performance should have been impressive. Ray Mallock was drafted in to share driving duties with Bernard de Dryver and Mario Hytten, the Briton putting in the best qualifying lap of 2min 31.20sec, 19th fastest, after a multitude of teething problems, including overheating. The latter problem was to occur again in the race when Mallock was lying 12th, and was then followed by gear selection troubles before eventually the crankshaft damper parted company with the V8, ending the Cheetah-Aston's maiden run.

Two weeks later, at Imola, the Cheetah was plagued with engine failures during practice, only managing to qualify 20th with a time of 1min 53.63sec, after which a broken camshaft

The EMKA-Aston Martin was considerably revised for the 1985 season. At Le Mans it again won the *Motor Trophy* as the first British car home.

prevented it starting the race. The car, however, was still not fully sorted, and over the winter considerable changes were made, including widening the body to the maximum width allowed and enlarging the underbody tunnels. The twin side radiators were replaced by a single unit in the nose, which cured the overheating, though all these modifications added around 25kg in weight.

The Cheetah-Aston was entered at Mugello in April for the first round of the 1985 WEC, the regulations of which had now reduced the fuel allowance by 15%. De Dryver and Gianfranco Brancatelli shared the driving duties, but it was not a good event for them. After minor engine problems the Cheetah qualified 13th in 1min 59.42sec, jamming throttle slides then delaying it early in the race before a detached rear wing caused its retirement with only a few laps completed. At Monza it was to fare even worse. Having qualified 18th with a 1min 51.52sec lap, right behind the C2 Ecosse of Ray Mallock, Brancatelli retired after three laps with apparent electrical failure – investigation afterwards revealed he'd merely knocked off the master switch! The Ecosse car, incidentally, was run by Richard Williams and that year it won the C2 championship; it was this Ecosse/Williams combination that effectively led to the subsequent formation of the Group C Aston Martin team.

The EMKA-Aston was to make its comeback at the Silverstone 1,000kms in May with the same driving trio as at Le Mans two years earlier, the Cheetah also appearing with John Cooper sharing with John Brindley. The EMKA had benefited from the removal of its underbody ground effects, a redesigned rear suspension and some substantial backing from silicon products manufacturer Dow Corning. In practice it out-qualified the Cheetah-Aston, Needell posting 17th fastest time with 1min 20.75sec against Cooper's 1min 26.09sec, 24th fastest. In the race, the Anglo/Swiss machine suffered first from more errant bodywork and then starter motor and rear suspension failure, the last ailment causing its retirement. Coincidentally, the EMKA also retired later with rear suspension failure.

The following month things were very different at Le Mans when the EMKA, with Needell driving, having qualified 13th with a time of 3min 33.12sec (the same as Mallock's Nimrod in 1984), actually led the race after an hour's racing, ahead of all the Porsches and the 630bhp Group 44 Jaguar XJR5s! It was a relatively short-lived but nevertheless stirring sight for British and Aston fans. Meanwhile, the Cheetah-Aston, with de Dryver sharing with Cooper and Claude Bourgoignie, had qualified 21st at 3min 58.33sec, again troubled by minor faults. It was also slow along Mulsanne, clocking only 183mph against the EMKA's 216mph. Problems persisted in the race, and ultimately the car crashed after almost five hours although by then its performance had improved and its potential was becoming evident. The EMKA and remaining Jaguar continued to battle together well into the 24-hour event until both had long pit stops, the former with clutch hydraulic problems. Thereafter the EMKA ran strongly, taking 11th place at the flag ahead of the 13th-place Jaguar, once again netting the *Motor* Trophy as the first British car across the line. With better reliability and two drivers with Needell's speed, who knows where the EMKA-Aston Martin

might otherwise have finished.

Needell was to change cars at Hockenheim in July, joining John Cooper in the Cheetah as the EMKA was not entered. This time fuel and suspension problems prevented the car qualifying higher than 20th, and in the race piston failure caused retirement. Chuck Greamiger, understandably, was not happy with the Tickford-built engines, having suffered various failures, especially with starter motors, and particularly after an independent dyno test showed as little as 498bhp against Tickford's claimed 580bhp. For these reasons, Graemiger opted to prepare his own engine for the Spa 1,000kms in September, where Pierre Dieudonné was paired with de Dryver. Using a new rear wing, de Dryver qualified the Cheetah ahead of the EMKA in 2min 20.33sec, half a second ahead of Needell, this time co-driving with O'Rourke and James Weaver, although the EMKA was suffering from understeer and power loss.

In the race, the tables were turned when the EMKA

Pit stop for the Anglo-Swiss Cheetah-Aston Martin at Le Mans the same year. It crashed in the fourth hour.

The Tickford Aston V8 engine was a neat installation in the Cheetah-Aston Martin.

retired with fuel pressure problems after leading the Cheetah, which went on to take 10th place, its best result ever. Both cars appeared at the Brands Hatch round in September, by which time Dow Corning had withdrawn its sponsorship following the crash that claimed Stefan Bellof's life at Spa. The EMKA thus had greater backing from Tickford, and Needell and O'Rourke this time were joined by Mark Galvin, with Hervé Regout sharing the Cheetah with de Dryver and Brindley.

A dropped valve in an apparently more powerful Tickford V8 hindered the EMKA in practice before Needell qualified 10th in 1min 23.98sec, using an old engine, against de Dryver's best in the Cheetah of 1min 24.95sec, which was good enough for 12th spot. In the race, the Cheetah was once again in trouble, this time with a leaking metering unit in the fuel injection system. The EMKA, however, climbed as high as fourth before it was delayed, first by a rear suspension breakage and then by water pump drive belt failure that ultimately caused its retirement in its last ever race. Soon after, a broken hub also caused the Cheetah's retirement. It was disappointing all round, not least for Tickford, who had been hopeful of a strong showing, but whose engines were plagued with unreliability.

The Cheetah-Aston was to do one more championship race at Fuji in October, de Dryver on this occasion being partnered by Laurent Ferrier. The Brands Hatch engine had been rebuilt by Tickford while the team remained in England, but after it began to sound unhealthy during the very wet practice it was changed for the Spa engine, the Cheetah then qualifying 26th after losing its rear bodywork! The race, however, proved to be a complete washout and most drivers opted to retire on safety grounds, amongst them de Dryver and Ferrier. Chuck Greamiger subsequently sold the Cheetah-Aston after losing his Gatoil sponsorship, and its new owner Jon Salmona then competed with it in German Supercup races.

There were to be no more Aston Martin V8-engined sportscars in the World Championship until May 1988, with the debut of the all-new AMR1. There was a marked difference, however, in that the AMR1 was 100% an Aston Martin and as such the first factory racing Aston Martin since 1963; the project had been brewing under the surface for some time in the minds of the parties concerned.

CHAPTER 8

V8 engine in competition – 3

AMR1 and a new factory team

While the Nimrod saga had hit hard the finances of those involved, Victor Gauntlett still maintained the desire to see the marque race once again at Le Mans, a sentiment strongly shared by both Peter Livanos and Richard Williams. But this time, it was decided, the proposed race car would be an Aston Martin in its entirety, rather than another manufacturer's chassis using an Aston engine. The decision to go ahead was finally taken in 1986, the year Hugh McCaig's Ecurie Ecosse team won the WEC's C2 category under Richard Williams' management. It seemed a natural choice for Ecurie Ecosse to be given the development contract to produce the new Aston contender, code number AMR1, the Scottish équipe in effect then being to Aston what TWR was to Jaguar. It was agreed, however, that the decision to race would only be taken if the car proved competitive during testing.

It was shortly after the official announcement of the AMR1 project in August 1987 that Ford became a 75% shareholder in Aston Martin Lagonda and Gauntlett was keen to stress at the time that the takeover was totally unrelated to motor racing of any kind. The American giant, however, gave its blessing to AMR1 only provided that no funds were forthcoming from within AML. That was, and continued to be, the case and it was AML shareholder Livanos himself who put up the £26 million budget to cover the project through a six-year period. He, like Gauntlett and Williams, would far rather win at Le Mans than the championship itself, indeed Le Mans was the team's main raison d'être.

To achieve that goal the design of the new Aston had to be state-of-the-art and, conceived by Max Boxstrom, formerly with Brabham, who had assisted with the Ecosse C2 car and was proprietor of Dymag Wheels (supplier to many GP teams), the resultant chassis was far more advanced than anything in Group C during the 1989 season. What he produced was a quite radical design, making the utmost use of ground effect within the strict (renamed) World Sports Prototype Championship regulations. The tub's construction used carbon and Kevlar composite skins for its three main components – the outer shell, floor and seat back panel – whereas most designs use a number of separate panels. All the bodywork was manufactured in a similar way using carbon-fibre moulds.

The heart of the AMR1 is thus a carbon/Kevlar central tub with a 'coke bottle' shape, similar to a Grand Prix single-seater, with a wide aerofoil under the nose. Air entering the nose, and pressing down on the aerofoil to create downforce, exits through large ducts forward of the doors, around the neck of the 'bottle', and in producing ground effect at the front of the car the Aston was to be unique amongst Group C machines. Another radical and very advanced aspect of the AMR1 is its stumpy rear, which features a very wide underbody venturi or tunnel, while above, a large adjustable wing creates suitable downforce, and under it is mounted the large twin water radiators, something of a novelty. Front and rear body sections and the doors clip simply and quickly to the main tub.

To accommodate the venturi, both the engine and gearbox, which also act as a stressed member, are notably inclined, a bonus being that the transaxle has most of its height forward of the axle line. The latter, incidentally, is not, as is usual, an

The four-valve version of Aston's trusty V8 waiting to receive its ancillaries in the prototype AMR1.

off-the-shelf item, but rather an in-house unit designed and built by Aston Martin. Using unequal-length driveshafts, it is an integral part of the car's design. So is the engine, although the trusty Aston V8 has been developed in four-valve form by Callaway Engineering in Connecticut, USA. Chosen on the merits of time, and experience with four-valve heads for racing applications, Callaway had already been commissioned to design the new 32-valve cylinder heads for the Virage (see chapter 12), so it was natural to continue development for the larger-capacity AMR1 powerplant. The 6-litre unit, which was used throughout the 1989 season bar the last race, is believed to have been producing 670 to 700bhp and around 500lb/ft of torque, though exact figures are kept under wraps.

For the suspension, unequal-length wishbones are used all round with coil spring/damper units, outboard at the front and inboard at the rear. Naturally, the ball-jointed suspension is fully adjustable, as are anti-roll bars front and rear. Initially, the new sportscar weighed a not inconsiderable 990kg, well above the minimum 900kg allowed under WSPC rules, but during the season this was progressively pared off to just over 900 kilos. The AMR1 is also sophisticated inside the cockpit, featuring digital readouts for various engine parameters and tyre temperatures with full telemetry equipment allowing constant monitoring of the car's functions throughout a race.

Although the prototype Aston, chassis AMR1/01, had a successful maiden run on November 28, 1988, it was to be January 1989 before the project was given the official green light to race, the announcement including the exciting news that the project would cover five years and thus change to the maximum-permitted 3.5-litre capacity for the 1991 season. The formation of two companies was also announced, Aston Martin Racing Development Project Ltd and Proteus Technology Ltd (Protech), the former to oversee AMR1 development and the latter the racing programme itself from a new fully equipped 37,000sq ft headquarters in Milton Keynes. Proteus had Livanos as majority shareholder with the remainder split equally between Williams and Ray Mallock, who also represented Ecurie Ecosse interests.

It was with some apprehension that the fledgling Aston team gave the AMR1 its debut at the Dijon round of the WSPC in May, 1989, having missed the opening 1989 round at Suzuka after a rear hub failure at Donington Park during testing, which had heavily damaged the prototype tub. Its absence from Japan cost Proteus a £250,000 fine, despite pleading *force majeure* due to a second chassis being far from ready to race. At Dijon, AMR1/02 had never run more than 20 laps at race speed before taking part in its first event in France. However, any worries proved ill-founded, the Mobil-liveried Aston running faultlessly, although it was clearly evident to drivers David Leslie and Brian Redman that an excess of downforce was limiting both straightline and cornering speeds. Having qualified 18th with a time of 1min 14.58sec, against the pole-position Sauber-Mercedes' 1min 7.27sec, the AMR1 was to finish 17th. While the placing was nothing to shout about, the Aston had proved its reliability in the 480-kilometre event (this distance replacing the old

AMR1/02 about to start its pace lap at Dijon on its race debut in May 1989.

At Dijon the AMR1 was hampered by excessive downforce, but ran reliably to finish 17th.

1,000kms) and, just as importantly, shown that the right potential was there.

Two AMR1s were entered for Le Mans, much to the delight of the tens of thousands of British fans on their annual pilgrimage to La Sarthe, although chassis number AMR1/03 had to be granted a special dispensation to be last at scrutineering in order to allow the Proteus mechanics to finish building it! It was not discovered what it weighed due to faulty scales, but AMR1/02 was recorded at 980kg. That the Astons were far from fully sorted was reflected in the latter's qualifying time of 3min 34.08sec, 35th fastest, and AMR1/03's 3min 40.11sec, which was good enough for only 43rd on the grid – a Sauber-Mercedes had again taken pole position in 3min 15.04sec.

British fans, however, were not to be disappointed, both Astons performing well despite the cars' aerodynamics effectively creating a 'brick wall' on Mulsanne, limiting top speed to 218mph in comparison to the 240mph of the front runners. Unluckily, the AMR1 of Leslie, Mallock and David Sears retired early on Sunday with engine failure after running

Two AMR1s were entered for Le Mans in 1989. Here they receive last-minute attention before the start of the race.

AMR1/03 retired at Le Mans with engine failure after running without a rev-counter for several hours. Here it sits abandoned at Mulsanne Corner while AMR1/02 went on to finish 11th.

for several hours without a rev-counter as a result of an electrical fire behind the dashboard. However, the sister car, AMR1/02, of Redman, Michael Roe and Costas Los soldiered on, its thundering V8 never missing a deep beat, to take 11th overall and 10th in Group C, a commendable result in only its second race. Once again, the AMR1 had displayed solid reliability, an asset that was to become its forté throughout the year.

The Brands Hatch round of the WSPC provided the AMR1 with its best result, the sole Aston crossing the line a fine fourth overall, a fitting end to the first race in Britain by a factory Aston for 25 years. Leslie had qualified a new chassis, AMR1/04, now weighing 920kg and benefiting from extensive suspension modifications, 14th fastest in 1min 17.96sec while Redman put in some laps in a spare T-car, the first time the team had such a luxury. Admittedly, the car's fourth place was aided by a high rate of attrition, but it nonetheless beat the debutant turbocharged Jaguar XJR11, having already proved itself a match for the normally aspirated XJR9.

But the AMR1 was to prove less effective around Nürburgring's faster curves, managing to qualify only 21st

fastest in 1min 31.10sec after being slowed by a misfire. Carbon-fibre brakes were fitted to AMR1/04 for the first time in Germany and weight was now down to 916kg, but again top speed was lacking, the Aston finishing eighth in a race which highlighted the need for an improvement in fuel consumption. Development on this and other fronts was given priority at Proteus and it paid off when AMR1/04 and a new chassis, AMR1/05, appeared at Donington Park in September, the respective weights now down to 912 and 906kg. Leslie, sharing the new car with Roe, qualified 10th in 1min 22.20sec, but Sears, paired with Redman, netted only 20th place on the grid with 1min 24.79sec after concentrating on fuel consumption tests. In the race there was to be no high retirement rate as at Brands Hatch, but the two red, white and blue AMR1s were able to show their true mettle and finished a worthy and impressive sixth and seventh, having run on the pace throughout, Leslie and Roe leading home Redman and Sears, the latter's car suffering from a slipping clutch and a broken front anti-roll bar. Bearing in mind the AMR1's initial performance at Dijon, progress had been very rapid indeed.

Brands Hatch brought the AMR1's best result with an encouraging fourth place.

AMR1/05 heads AMR1/04 at Donington Park in 1989. They ran nose-to-tail for many laps, finishing in strong sixth and seventh places.

The surviving Aston Martin, AMR1/04, finished seventh at Spa-Francorchamps. AMR1/05's subsequent eighth place in the final Mexico round secured Aston Martin sixth place in the World Sports Prototype Championship.

After this competent showing, chassis 04 and 05 were both entered for the Spa round in September, Leslie sharing 04 with Roe while Redman in 05 was joined by Stanley Dickens, who had co-driven the Le Mans-winning Sauber-Mercedes. The Aston team, like many others, was thrown somewhat off-balance by the soaking practice conditions, the AMR1s never having run in the wet before and being plagued by water-related misfires. Once the cars were cured of this and a suitable suspension set-up reached, Leslie qualified 13th in 2min 17.08sec and Dickens a lowly 32nd in 2min 29.76sec after running out of fuel due to a vapour lock, which misled the team into believing the tank was full. Both cars, however, were caught out on intermediate tyres when the track started to dry, the fastest times being set on slicks. In the race, the leading Aston of Leslie and Roe was to suffer the team's first genuine engine breakage when running eighth, due to a connecting rod failure, but the surviving Redman and

Dickens machine went on to finish seventh. The Proteus crew were not too deterred by the demise of one of their V8s bearing in mind that several other teams, including Jaguar, had experienced many more engine failures than this.

The final round of the WSPC was held in Mexico, a sole Aston, AMR1/05, being entered for Leslie and Redman, with its weight down to 906kg and a lighter and more powerful Version II engine fitted. What that meant was a displacement of 6.3 rather than 6 litres and more power and torque, the V8 having been further developed by Callaway under Richard Williams' guidance. Detailed output figures were not released, but 740bhp at 7,750rpm and around 550lb/ft of torque were on tap. It was not, however, to be much help in Mexico, the altitude of almost 7,000ft robbing the Aston V8 of up to 20% of its power, unlike the turbocharged cars, with which it was far easier to adapt settings. The AMR1 was also hampered by excessive drag, again limiting top speed, and Leslie was only able to qualify in 15th position with a time of 1min 27.18sec. Nonetheless, it ran with utter reliability and finished eighth overall, good enough to place the Aston Martin team sixth in the world championship, not at all a bad result from the car's first season.

Over the winter of 1989/90 much work was carried out on the AMR1, Ray Mallock having taken over the car's design following Max Boxstrom's departure early in the season to concentrate on his wheel business. It was the intention that a new evolutionary AMR1 with much improved aerodynamics would fly the Aston flag for the first half of the season, with a new AMR2 model joining the fray for a three-car assault on Le Mans, by which time a Version III engine might also be in use. The reliability was already there and it's fair to say that had the 1989 races been to the old 1,000kms distance rather than 480kms, the Aston Martin team would probably have been a regular top-three finisher. With two new packages prepared for 1990 the potential for success looked to be vastly increased, but early in the new year came the shock news that the race programme had been shelved due to Ford's withdrawal of its 3.5-litre F1 engine for the 1991 season and uncertainty over the running of the 1990 Le Mans race. Under Ford ownership there were now other priorities for the company and its resources and at the time of writing it is impossible to predict when, or whether, Aston Martin will return to Le Mans.

CHAPTER 9

V8 Vantage

In the best of traditions

Judging by the previous Aston Martin models available in Vantage specification, the company was a little slow in producing a Vantage version of the V8, but bearing in mind the various financial crises and management reshuffles that preceded it, perhaps it was lucky it appeared as early as February 18, 1977. It had long been evident that the V8, now in Series 3 form, could comfortably cope with considerably more horsepower than the 304bhp of the standard car, and the launch of the V8 Vantage coincided nicely from a marketing point of view with the entry of Robin Hamilton's heavily modified DBS V8 at Silverstone in May and Le Mans in June the same year. Indeed, Hamilton still argues that it was his race car that gave Aston the idea for the Vantage's body shape after he had suggested in 1975 that the factory produce a limited-edition V8 based on the Le Mans car with a power output of between 380 and 400bhp. His idea was that the factory could invest £20,000 in his Le Mans project by loading the price by £1,000 a vehicle; the idea was rejected, but perhaps it did plant an extra seed from which the similarly conceived Vantage was to grow.

The public was unwittingly treated to an early glimpse of the V8 Vantage's likely performance at Silverstone in June 1976 when Mike Loasby demonstrated a very rapid V8 at the annual AMOC St John Horsfall meeting. When the Vantage did appear, beginning with chassis number V8/11563/RCAV – the V for Vantage) it sported a neat but separate boot spoiler, a deeper front air dam, a blanked-off radiator grille and bonnet air scoop (to force cooling air under the bumper), Perspex covers for the headlamps, stiffer suspension with

Koni dampers, and wider 255/60-section Pirelli CN12 tyres on the standard 7in wide wheels. The most important differences, of course, were hidden under the bonnet, the V8 producing around 380bhp at 6,000rpm (figures, as usual, were not released) or approximately 40% more power, with an extra 10% of torque at around 380lb/ft at 4,000rpm, through revised camshafts, larger inlet valves, quadruple 48 IDF downdraught Weber carburettors on a special manifold and a different airbox. As such, Aston Martin claimed the V8 Vantage to be the fastest production vehicle in the world – once the claim of the lighter DBS V8 – something other supercar manufacturers found hard to disprove. Mated to the standard five-speed ZF gearbox (at least three automatic V8 Vantages were produced, but officially these were not available due to worries regarding the strength of the Torqueflite transmission), the car had been timed at 5.3sec from 0 to 60mph, just 12.7sec from 0 to 100mph and on to a top speed of 170mph, hence the need for the body's aerodynamic accoutrements.

The press, as well as eager customers, were keen to find out if the V8 Vantage was really as quick as claimed. In April 1978, a month after production had started, *Motor Sport* soon confirmed the 5.3 seconds to 60mph time while *Autocar* managed 5.4sec and 13sec for the 100mph sprint with an estimated top speed of 170mph. *Motor*, however, could manage no better than 5.8sec to 60mph, a slightly improved 12.9sec to 100mph, but a very poor (and dubious) top speed of 148mph, little better than the standard V8. Depending on whose figures one believes, the V8 Vantage was, or was

The prototype V8 Vantage was actually a V8 converted in December 1976. Here chassis number V8/11470/RCAC makes a timed run at an AMOC Curborough sprint. Note the blanked-off grille and intake, Perspex lamp covers and separate tail spoiler.

This early V8 Vantage was an experimental factory car fitted with automatic transmission.

VNK 349S also took part in the 1979 Grosvenor House Beaujolais Run, pictured here with the winning Series 4 AM V8.

A Series 2 V8 Vantage poses at the 1981 Dubai GP.

almost, the fastest production car in the world, and there seems little chance the truth will ever be known, so close were its times to those of other exotica and so dependent were these times on the variables of test conditions and drivers behind the relevant wheels. There was little doubt, though, that no other car would get past the Vantage, nor would any car ahead lose the Aston. With so much power and torque in hand, its handling was exemplary for such a large car and very predictable, its steering response crisp, traction excellent, brakes reassuringly effective and, unlike the others, the £20,000 V8 Vantage was the only full four-seater.

Once the Series 4 'Oscar India' V8 superseded the Series 3, the V8 Vantage was altered accordingly into Series 2 form, both cars now featuring the Vantage rear boot spoiler as an integral part of the rear wings and bootlid though less severe in rake than the separate spoiler of the original V8 Vantage. There were, however, no mechanical changes to the V8 Vantage bar a slight improvement in torque, performance remaining as before, though with the new-style Series 4 chassis numbers, Vantages became identifiable by the second

The integral tail spoiler of the Series 2 V8 Vantage is clear in this shot.

A V8 Vantage Series 1 cornering hard at Silverstone.

V in, for example, the chassis number of the first Series 2 car produced in October 1978, V8VOR 12040. *Motor* tested a Series 2 Vantage in its April 25, 1981 issue, obtaining far better results than with the Series 1, recording the 0 to 60mph dash in 5.2sec and 0 to 100mph in just 11.9sec.

No changes were made to the Vantage until it appeared in Series 3 guise at the Birmingham Motor Show in October 1986, the price now having risen to £59,500, around £5,000 more expensive than the standard V8. Power was increased through higher-lift camshafts, larger ports and a compression ratio raised from 9.5 to 10.2:1, and now that Aston Martin was revealing power figures, 400bhp was claimed with the temptation of a 432bhp option with no less than 395lb/ft of torque at 5,100rpm, the latter from the same specification as the V8 Vantage Zagato (see next chapter) with the extra power derived from using 50mm Webers and a larger-bore exhaust system. Production of these cars, which like the Series 5 V8 had 16in diameter wheels and new-style chassis numbers with Vantage specification identified by a V prefix rather than a V suffix while those with the 432bhp option

The Series 3 V8 Vantage at its Castle Ashby launch in late 1986.

Malcolm Young's Series 2 V8 Vantage complete with detuned 446bhp Nimrod-Aston engine. A very rapid road machine!

have an X prefix, finally ended in December 1989 once Virage production had got underway.

The V8 Vantage is a truly fast and enjoyable supercar, built in the best of Aston Martin traditions and combining all the virtues the marque is famous for. However, some people have to go one better and I must make mention of one of my favourite road Astons, the subtly modified V8 Vantage of AMOC member Malcolm Young which I tested for *Autocar* magazine in 1987 – and which I have been fortunate to drive several times since. Hidden under its dark blue bonnet is nothing less than one of Tickford's Nimrod-Aston Martin engines, albeit detuned through altered camshaft profiles and different induction, but nonetheless producing an installed 446bhp at 6,250rpm with mammoth torque of 407lb/ft at 5,000rpm. Suitably registered 1 AMT, the car is also lowered and runs on 16in x 8in BBS alloy wheels with similarly-sized Goodyear Eagle tyres to the later V8 Vantage and V8 Vantage Zagato models. In conjunction with lowered and stiffened suspension, which doesn't sacrifice the ride, it is a superb-handling machine. Body modifications have been limited to

This Series 1 V8 Vantage has a 6.3-litre prototype version of the two-valve V8 motor developed by RS Williams. It produces around 450bhp with tremendous torque, and the capacity change was to become a popular factory option.

subtle sill skirts blended neatly with the front air dam and rear valance, but all most drivers are likely to see is a blur of blue. On a damp surface I recorded 0 to 60mph in 4.52sec and 0 to 100mph in 12.4sec, while the car's top speed is between 175 and 180mph. Now that is a V8 Vantage with which other exotics really will have trouble keeping up!

One other V8 Vantage that must be mentioned was initially developed by Aston specialist Richard Williams, later manager of the factory's Group C sportscar team. As mentioned in the previous chapter, for the final race of 1989 a 6.3 rather than a 6-litre version of the four-valve Aston V8 was used. This capacity, however, had first been experimented with in a roadgoing Vantage, albeit in two-valve form, which when Williams closed his business to concentrate on the race team, was taken over by the factory. Producing 465bhp and with even greater torque than Malcolm Young's V8 Vantage –

450lb/ft – such an engine conversion was offered as a factory option on both new and older V8 models. Concurrently a handling kit was offered complete with altered steering geometry, revised spring rates and roll bar settings and stiffer Koni dampers. By May 1990, having been introduced late the previous year, 24 6.3 engine conversions had been completed or ordered, including V8 Vantage Zagato models, though at a cost of £25,000 to £30,000, dependent on the condition of the V8 in 5.3-litre form, it was not a cheap option. The handling kit was available at £3,500. Having briefly driven the development car, registered 7 EXY (and commonly known as SEXY), which has performance on a par with the Tickford-engined car, I suggest these V8 Vantages must be ones to look out for in years to come. Certainly they must be the fastest factory-built four-seaters ever.

CHAPTER 10

V8 Vantage Zagato

Limited edition revives the past

One of the most sought-after roadgoing Aston Martins of all time is the DB4 GT Zagato built between 1960 and 1962, a lightweight coupé specially designed by Zagato to finally beat the Ferrari 250 GTOs that dominated sportscar racing in the late 'fifties/early 'sixties. Only 19 examples (all differing slightly in bodywork style) were produced, and today these highly desirable Astons fetch astronomical prices. Rapidly joining them in the so-called investment stakes – much to the detriment of true enthusiasts who would use these cars rather than hide them in heated garages – is the limited-edition V8 Vantage Zagato, an Aston which the factory planned would take its place right at the top of the supercar league through using the Vantage running gear and a 432bhp engine in a totally new and much lighter bodyshell. It was an aim that was achieved.

For some time Victor Gauntlett had considered renewing the old relationship between Aston Martin and Zagato, the famous Italian coachbuilder, and he and Peter Livanos duly approached brothers Gianni and Dr Elio Zagato to discuss the possibility at the Geneva Motor Show in March 1984. The basic requirements were a top speed of 300km/h (187mph) and a sub-5sec 0 to 60mph time, and in July 1984 Giuseppe Mittino, Zagato's chief stylist, visited Newport Pagnell, at the same time delivering a proposed body design and acquiring chassis details of the current V8 from which to draw up a suitable basis for the new car, which would have at least a 10% weight saving over the V8 Vantage. One year after those initial discussions at Geneva, the V8 Vantage Zagato was displayed at the same venue; it was Aston

Martin's first roadgoing two-seater since the DB4 GT Zagato. Four months later, at about the time the first V8 Vantage Zagato was delivered, AML was to acquire a 50% shareholding in Zagato (one part of AML, incidentally, that was not part of the deal when Ford took over majority shares in AML in late 1987).

Zagato had calculated that a drag coefficient of 0.29 would be needed with 432bhp and a 3.06:1 final-drive ratio in the limited-slip differential to achieve the required performance, while Aston Martin decided to sell in advance the 50 cars that would be produced. There was no difficulty in finding enough people to part with the necessary £30,000 deposit towards the £87,000 asking price.

Several prospective customers were flown to Zagato's Milan headquarters to see the prototype and some of them disliked the body shape; admittedly, it could be described as bland in comparison with some of the mid-engined exotica with which it competes. But the shape is clean, neat and easy on the eye, at the same time exuding an aggressive air and subtle poise, the only real criticism being the unsightly bonnet bulge, which was larger on the prototype than on the production cars, but necessary to clear the 50 IDF Weber carburettors (using bored-out 48mm chokes) and new twin plenum chambers. Fuel injection would have negated the need for the bulge, but then less than 432bhp would have been available, insufficient power to achieve the 300km/h top speed Aston had already publicly trumpeted.

The final production V8 Vantage Zagatos – running from chassis number V8ZGR 20010 to V8ZJR 20062 (excluding

The V8 Vantage Zagato was capable of 186mph with its 432bhp engine and 10% weight saving over the V8 Saloon. At £87,000 in October 1986 it was also very expensive, but nonetheless an extremely desirable machine.

The original clay model of the V8 Vantage Zagato.

The chassis of the second Aston model with body by Zagato was the same as the V8's, but with chopped-off rear overhang.

Victor Gauntlett and the Zagato brothers with one of the first Zagatos completed.

20042) – while retaining the V8's 8ft 6¾in wheelbase, are 11¼in shorter overall at 14ft 4¾in, the majority of this reduction achieved by chopping off most of the V8's overhang beyond the rear wheels. Width is fractionally more at 6ft 1¾in and height exactly 4ft 3in with a weight saving of 370lb over the V8 Vantage, the Zagato version tipping the scales at 3,637lb. All the Zagatos were bodied and built by the Milanese concern, AML sending out a rolling platform chassis complete with all V8 Vantage mechanicals which had already been rolling road-tested at Newport Pagnell – though with the 16in x 8in BBS wheels replaced by the Zagato's unique and attractive Speedline rims. Zagato would then add its own superstructure on which to mount the body panels in a similar way to Aston's own build method.

Naturally, the aluminium body was beautifully finished, with all glass a flush fit to assist in obtaining the 0.29 Cd, while two spoilers at the rear, on the bootlid and at the tip of the rear valance, and a bib spoiler at the front, helped to produce 120lb of downforce at 150mph. The aerodynamics were calculated and achieved using a Computer Aided Design (CAD) system, once a quarter-scale model had been constructed, the accuracy of the original calculations being confirmed by the CAD's first Cd reading of 0.286. Rather than have bumpers, the V8 Vantage Zagato uses deformable, separate panelling at each end made from polyurethane foam-covered glass-reinforced polyester (GRP), while the radiator grille retains the traditional Aston Martin shape. Another traditional feature is the Zagato 'double blister' trademark on the roof.

In the spring of 1988 I was fortunate enough to have the use of Victor Gauntlett's own V8 Vantage Zagato (chassis number V8ZHR 20046) in order to write a comparison between this ultimate Aston Martin road car and the Ulster, the marque's ultimate prewar machine. By this time, having once failed at Le Mans to achieve the promised 187mph top speed after fuel problems had embarrassingly intervened, the Zagato had officially been clocked at 298.75km/h (185.63mph) at a second attempt with 0 to 60mph achieved

The Zagato's tail spoiler helped both stability and the achievement of its 0.29 Cd. Note the double-Z badging on the bootlid.

Here the works development V8 Vantage Zagato shares the track with a 1935 Aston Martin 1½-litre Mk II.

The V8 Vantage Zagato on parade alongside one of its forebears, a DB4GT Zagato, outside the Aston Martin Lagonda offices in Newport Pagnell on the day of the new car's launch.

in 4.8sec, good enough to satisfy honour.

I had been dubious of the appeal of the Zagato when painted in certain light colours, but the Aston chairman's example was resplendent in dark metallic Hunter Green and looked quite magnificent, the colour setting off the Italianate lines superbly. Inside, all was red leather and the quality of the trim excellent, though the Italian stitching on the seats and facia, in comparison to Aston's own, left a little to be desired if any criticism at all is to be made. The Aston chairman's pride and joy also boasted a beautiful Nardi wood-rim wheel which perfectly set off the interior, far more so than the black leather-rim item fitted as standard to the other 49 examples.

Out on the open road (when that bonnet bulge became a complete insignificance), the Vantage Zagato was a revelation, offering some of the most surefooted manners of any supercar. The 432bhp was quite capable of delivering the promised performance, flooring the throttle being answered with snorts from the big Webers and a demented dance from the tachometer needle. Acceleration was electric, really coming into its own at 120mph and above, and while I did not take any figures, it certainly felt to be in the sub-5sec bracket from rest to 60mph, with 170mph quite literally a 'piece of cake'. The large ventilated disc brakes were well up to the job of stopping 32.5cwt, albeit after solid pressure is applied to the pedal, but once warm they were most reassuring, though there was a tendency to weave when braking very hard.

The gearchange was also a revelation after similarly equipped V8s and V8 Vantages, and quite simply the best ZF I've encountered on a road car – precise, baulk-free and with no hint of slack, though when hot the usual layshaft rattle at idle was still evident. Understeer was minimal enough to be non-existent, and a lot of persuasion was needed to make the rear end break away, the huge 255-section tyres and limited-slip differential providing tenacious grip despite the torque. There was plenty of warning when the rear did break, the Aston then responding obediently and without drama to the necessary steering and throttle inputs. Quite simply, the V8 Vantage Zagato was a fantastically enjoyable and satisfying car, justifiably at the top of the supercar league with its incredible all-round performance; Victor Gauntlett was lucky that I returned it!

After the successful sell-out of the closed Zagato – and the exorbitant prices being paid by those desperate to get their hands on one – AML decided to produce another limited edition of 25 convertible models, this time priced at £125,000 apiece. The first of these Aston Martin V8 Volante Zagato models was displayed at the Geneva Show in March 1987, but it was actually one of the 50 coupés, V8ZJR 20042, converted to convertible to become V8XGR 20042. Demand, however, saw the production run increased to 35, the remaining chassis numbers then running from V8ZJR 30010 to V8ZKR 30043. Apart from the lack of a roof, the other notable difference was a non-Vantage specification engine which, through employing the standard V8's fuel

The Volante Zagato's stepped head-lamps exposed on the top level of the three-tier lighting layout. The radiator intake is recessed between the nose spoiler and the main bumper panel.

Open-air elegance. The beautifully furnished cockpit of the V8 Volante Zagato. Note the position of the handbrake, to the left of the steering column on this right-hand-drive car.

It pays to take care when reversing a V8 Volante Zagato because, as at the front, there is no real protection from the impact of other cars' bumpers and overriders. The car is equipped with a de Dion rear axle.

injection system, meant that the unsightly bonnet bulge could be dispensed with. The car was also around 35kg heavier than the coupé through the need for additional strengthening below the waistline to compensate for the loss of rigidity with the roof removed. A new, and less attractive, radiator grille distinguishes the convertible from the front, while matching 'eyelids' cover the headlamps when not in use, which increases the Volante Zagato's length by 3¾in over its closed counterpart to 14ft 8½in. Width is the same at 6ft 1¼in and height just ¼in more at 4ft 3¼in. The drag factor was claimed to be similar to the Vantage Zagato, but at over half a hundredweight heavier at 33.1cwt, and with well over 100bhp less, the performance was similar to the V8 Volante with 0 to 60mph claimed in 6sec and a top speed of 160mph. Several V8 Volante Zagatos were subsequently returned to the factory to have the 432bhp engine and the closed car's front panel fitted, making them probably the world's fastest ever convertible production car.

CHAPTER 11

Bulldog and other specials

Prototypes and one-offs

In 1976, during the early development stages of the new Lagonda, itself an ambitious project, thoughts at Aston Martin – in particular Alan Curtis' – had turned to a mid-engined concept car, a high-performance, high-technology supercar that would serve as an example of Aston's craftsmanship and engineering expertise. Ultimately to be called Bulldog, the plan was that a working prototype be displayed at the 1978 Birmingham Motor Show, but when work on the Lagonda suffered various setbacks, so too did Bulldog, which was temporarily put on the back burner. Indeed, it was surprising that Bulldog was ever started, bearing in mind both the difficult financial situation at Newport Pagnell and the problems with finalizing the new Lagonda for production – and yet at the same time Aston Martin managed to find time to design and launch a Volante version of the V8!

Under engineering manager Mike Loasby, work had begun on the then unnamed Bulldog project, chassis number V8 TSLM, in 1977, William Towns drawing a startling, two-seat wedge design complete with huge gullwing doors. However, once Loasby had left the Aston fold to join De Lorean, his successor Steve Coughlin took over the Bulldog project and he in turn passed responsibility to products manager Keith Martin with development engineer Steve Hallam. Martin took over a semi-complete car, now bearing the code DP K901 (DP for Development Project, while K9 started the canine connection), and he and his team were allocated a secluded area of the factory that was soon christened The Kennel, out of which just 12 months later emerged the finished Bulldog.

On April 15, 1980, Bulldog was revealed to the press, a very low and wide symmetrical wedge design with a steeply-raked windscreen, large glass area and concave, power-operated gullwing doors which, when open, stood at 6ft 3in, allowing easy access to the luxurious interior. The doors also required a 9ft wide gap if both were to be opened together. They were operated by four push-buttons located in a panel beneath the quarter-light window, but manual operation was possible in the event of the hydraulic system failing. The windscreen was also innovative. Specially produced by Triplex, using a gas hearth process, the screen was said to be completely devoid of distortion, with its curvature running in only one direction. Its single 26in wiper was also specially designed to sweep a 145-degree arc using a six-bar linkage. Rather than mar the Bulldog's lines with hydraulically operated flip-up headlights, a battery of five Lagonda units was hidden behind the electrically operated front 'bonnet' panel.

The car's length was 15ft 6in, its height 3ft 7in and width a considerable 6ft 3½in, while the overall weight was 3,200lb. Whether one considered the Bulldog's looks attractive was definitely a matter of personal taste, but it has to be said that, lacking any flowing lines, the shape was somewhat bland. Under the skin there were many innovative ideas such as four separate but symmetrically interlinked fuel tanks, two main tanks plus two wedge-shaped units behind the rear passenger bulkhead, which, like the front bulkhead, was fireproofed and lined with special Vernaware insulating material. The tanks were so positioned that a diminishing fuel load did not upset the car's handling balance, and they were foam-filled, as required for competition cars, this being a precaution against tank explosion in the event of an accident. Several components such as the radiator were mounted at an angle to facilitate the car's low height, and with a Cd of just 0.34 it was hoped Bulldog would be capable of 200mph.

Providing the power to attain such a speed was a mid-mounted, twin-turbocharged version of the Aston V8, using much of the experience gained with the similarly powered Lagonda and bearing the engine number V8 TMDP K901 – there was also, incidentally, a stillborn twin-turbo racing marine version. In the Bulldog application, which used Bosch, DBS V8-derived fuel injection to keep the rear body panel as low as possible, Aston claimed power was no less than 60% up on the V8 Vantage when the twin Garrett TO4B turbochargers, mounted either side of the V8, were running at maximum boost. That equates to about 590bhp at 6,000rpm, while an educated guess might put the maximum torque figure at around 550 to 600lb/ft at 5,500rpm. A wastegate on each exhaust manifold limited boost pressure to 12psi, while modified DBS V8 plenum chambers and throttle bodies delivered air to twin quartets of ram pipes and the fuel injectors themselves. Special forged, flat-top Cosworth pistons limited the compression ratio to 7.5:1.

To keep the wet-sump V8 cool in the crowded engine bay, no less than 9 gallons of water circulated in the cooling system, running from the twin electric fan-assisted radiator via copper pipes within the cockpit's outer chassis rails. Ducting immediately forward of the rear wheelarches, on the car's underside, directed cooling air on to twin oil coolers, air also being directed around the engine bay and exiting via slats in the Bulldog's tail over the front part and low-pressure area of the rear window opening. This use of the high-pressure air beneath the car also helped to alleviate any tendency towards lift at high speed.

Mated to this lusty 5.3-litre engine by a 10.5in AP Racing clutch and an adaptor plate was a five-speed ZF transaxle with a high 3.20:1 final-drive ratio giving the 31.9mph per 1,000rpm necessary for the required top speed, but not high enough to worry the Aston V8 in the lower gears with such considerable torque. To make sure it would stop from 200mph (at which speed the Aston V8 would have to pull 6,300rpm in top gear) CanAm-type 11.67in x 1.25in ventilated disc brakes with four-pot calipers were fitted all round. The rear hubs, incidentally, used SKF's twin-row ball-race bearings, sealed for life, rather than the more usual tapered needle-roller type used for the front hubs.

In line with the current models, the Bulldog's multi-tubular chassis featured a de Dion, coil-sprung rear axle with parallel trailing arms and Watts linkage, though the ZF transaxle necessitated some rerouting of the latter, using solid-bushed lateral rods running from the hub carriers to L-shaped link bars. Any change in the length of the links, interconnected at a central point beneath the transaxle, was catered for by hard but flexible rubber bushes at the central pivot. A conventional unequal-length wishbone and coil spring set-up with adjustable anti-roll bar was used at the front, though apparently at one stage the car was to have had de Dion axles at both ends! Adjustable Koni dampers (for bump and rebound) were fitted all round and Compomotive split-rim alloy wheels, the trims of which featured blading designed to direct cooling air to the brakes, were used. These measured 8½in x 15in at the front, 11in x 15in at the rear, and were shod with fat 225/50 VR15 and 345/35 VR15 Pirelli P7 tyres (with a Michelin space-saver housed above the engine), the covers being specially buffed and X-rayed before fitment. The wheelbase measured 9ft 1in and front and rear tracks 5ft 1½in and 5ft 2½in, respectively. A modified DB6 rack provided 2¼ turns of the 13in leather-rimmed steering wheel from lock to lock, anti-Ackermann steering geometry was provided and there was no power-assistance.

The chassis also featured a built-in roll-over bar which with diagonal bracing was said to be very rigid, while the aluminium-panelled body was fixed to the usual lightweight steel frame. Inside the huge, hydraulically operated doors, passengers in the left-hand-drive' cockpit were treated to a sumptuous interior in Connolly hide, walnut burr and Wilton carpeting, although the tinted windows were non-opening. The instrumentation benefited from Lagonda-type sensors using six LCD (liquid crystal) readouts illuminated by a luminous strip drawing light from a central source via fibre optics.

At the April 15, 1980 press launch the attendant journalists were able to closely examine Bulldog, but in a brave move, considering the lack of testing miles on the car, Aston Martin had allowed some writers to test-drive it a few days earlier at both Mallory Park race circuit and the Motor Industry Research Association (MIRA) testing grounds. It was at the latter venue that Aston had hoped the Bulldog would prove its 200mph capability, though at this stage 172mph was the highest figure recorded, a maximum speed run having yet to be tried. However, the factory had attained 0 to 60mph and 0 to 100mph times of 5.1 and 10.1sec, respectively.

After its launch – the public had also had a first viewing at Compton Abbas Airfield on June 22 – work continued on perfecting Bulldog, including a redesigned exhaust system with the turbochargers repositioned more into the airstream to reduce the very high temperatures they had been reaching, this modification dropping the maximum temperature from 1,100°C to 950°C! At the same time, the twin oil coolers were similarly moved from their place immediately forward of each rear wheel and an adjustable anti-roll bar added to the rear suspension.

Much of the original Bulldog team, however, had been split up, some through the redundancies of the time or through reallocation to another department. Project manager Keith Martin then continued with Bulldog alone

Bulldog at its launch in April 1980. Its striking looks, gullwing doors and twin-turbocharged engine caused quite a stir. With both doors open a 9ft gap was needed.

Stirling Moss, who demonstrated the Bulldog at the 1980 St John Horsfall meeting, at speed past the pits at Silverstone. As this photograph suggests, rear vision was not one of the car's strong points, but a battery of five Lagonda headlamps, hidden behind an electrically operated flap in the nose, helped to show the way ahead after dark.

and it made appearances at the AMOC St John Horsfall meeting at Silverstone in June 1980, with Stirling Moss at the wheel, and at the 1980 Birmingham Motor Show and Cavalcade (being driven from the factory to the exhibition site by Martin himself).

Subsequently, over the winter of 1980, the engine was stripped down and after discovering some piston and ring damage due to an incorrect air filter allowing foreign particles to enter the induction system, and an over-rich mixture, it was decided to make a few modifications. New forged Cosworth pistons with increased skirt clearance and rings in EN31 steel were fitted, while the cylinder heads received enlarged ports and some new camshaft profiles that engine man Dave Morgan had developed for the marine version of the V8. The waterways linking heads and block were also enlarged to increase coolant flow and fine adjustments were made to the injection system's inlet tracts and the turbocharger wastegates. The result was an output of over 700bhp at 6,000rpm, enough to realize 207mph at 6,500rpm.

Further wind-tunnel testing revealed that while the Bulldog's shape was aerodynamically efficient, at 200mph it was producing over 900lb of lift. Fitting a front air dam reduced this to just 250lb, while fitting a rear spoiler reduced rear-end lift from 495lb to almost zero. Thereafter, several trips were made to MIRA where the acceleration proved shattering, 150mph being reached before the car had got into fourth gear. Nonetheless, the maximum speed ever reached was only 191mph, though in fairness MIRA's relatively short straights precluded going faster – given the right track, no doubt the Aston Martin Bulldog would have achieved its 200mph goal. One thing that it did achieve, as had been planned from the beginning, was considerable press and televison coverage, highlighting the skills and capabilities of Newport Pagnell. In the meantime, this very fast and unique Aston Martin is back in the UK having been sold by its original American purchaser.

Bulldog has been included first in this chapter because it was a prototype produced by Aston Martin itself, but there had been one-off vehicles produced independently that used the Aston Martin V8 engine and running gear. The first of these was the Siva 530, which won a styling exercise organized by the *Daily Telegraph* and was displayed at the 1971 Earls Court Motor Show. A mid-engined, lightweight coupé designed by Neville Trickett, its epoxy resin body was sleek and low and featured gullwing doors, but overall it was not aesthetically pleasing; being very modern was, perhaps, its saving grace. The interior, entered over high box sills, was strictly a two-seater with a space-age dashboard that featured a rectangular steering wheel. The Aston engine was said to be modified to give 350bhp, but there is no record of the Siva 530 ever having run and it was not seen again.

The following year, soon after the Siva's appearance, Ogle displayed a one-off special at the January 1972 Montreal Show using a standard DBS V8 chassis and running gear with manual transmission. Each year this show would feature dream cars from all over the world and in 1969 Ogle had been commissioned by the organizers to produce a British centrepiece that was a sophisticated, elegant and characterful fast car embodying new ideas yet was also a practical vehicle for the road.

David Ogle, founder of the Hertfordshire-based concern, had been killed in a car accident in 1962, but his partner, John Ogier, famous for his Essex Racing Stables Aston Martins and also a keen AMOC member, saw the Aston Martin DBS V8 as the ideal base for such a practical dream car. The resulting design, which was not started until 1971 under Tom Karen, featured an unusually styled glassfibre body with a high upswept tail, a low nose incorporating headlights hidden by flush-fitting, pneumatically operated shutters, and a very large glass area that included the whole roof. Some of the major panels – front and rear extremities and sills – were formed in brushed stainless steel with no less than 22 separate circular lights dominating the car's rear, including lights to indicate progressive braking – two lights for a gentle application, four for medium braking and six for hard applications. With backing from the tobacco company W D and H O Wills, the Ogle car was painted in its new Sotheby brand's dark blue and gold livery but, while AML had supplied the DBS V8 chassis and running gear – chassis number DBSV8/10381/RC – the company was keen that the Ogle car should not be known as an Aston Martin. After Montreal, the Ogle Aston went on display at both the Geneva

An array of Lagonda-type high-tech switchgear and display panels was incorporated into the driving compartment of the only Bulldog to be built, and the prototype car was furnished to a luxurious standard.

Motor Show in March 1972 and the Earls Court Motor Show the following October.

Heat-absorbent Triplex Sundym glass with a double curvature was employed, supported by a load-carrying tubular structure made from Reynolds 531 tubing. Inside, the Sotheby Special was a three-seater, with the single rear seat set diagonally across the car, trimmed in grey Connolly hide like the front seats, and complemented by a green corduroy-type material for the trim. Innovative features included Kangol seat belts that had to be in use before the car could be driven off and an array of warning lights that when illuminated flashed onto the windscreen in a head-up display just below the driver's line of sight. Overall, the Sotheby Special was only marginally larger than the DBS V8 upon which it was based, with a length of 15ft 6¾in, a width almost the same at 6ft 0½in and a height of 4ft 3⅞in, while weight was only slightly less at 34½cwt. Unlike the Siva, the Sotheby Special was a full roadgoing car capable of 160mph and both it, and a replica built in January 1973, are still in use today. The replica, incidentally, was built on an AM V8 chassis, number

V8/10581/RCA, but was fitted with automatic transmission, having been commissioned by an elderly lady living close to the Aston Martin factory who desired something different to the cars she regularly saw on test! A half-built display car without running gear is also said to have existed around the time of the Montreal Show, but its fate is not known.

Back in the days of the film *Goldfinger*, James Bond drove a gadget-equipped DB5, then, in *On Her Majesty's Secret Service*, agent 007 used a DBS Vantage. For a while, Aston Martins did not feature in the Bond films, but in 1987 the tradition was continued in *The Living Daylights*. In the film, Bond uses both a V8 Vantage and a V8 Volante, though viewers are led to believe that they are one and the same, the former actually being Victor Gauntlett's own car. Indeed, the film producers even asked Gauntlett to play the part of a KGB agent.

The pre-body skirt Vantage-specification Volante and specially equipped Vantage actually put the original Bond DB5 to shame with all their gadgetry. Rather than submachine guns, ace special equipment boffin Q had gone one

better and fitted missiles behind the sidelights, which could be aimed via a computerized control panel that sighted the target through a head-up display on the windscreen. There was bullet-proof glass all round and the extending spinners had been replaced by up-to-the-minute high-technology lasers, while the tyres had automatically operated spikes for snow and ice that could be retracted at the push of a button! And just to make the Vantage really versatile, another button produced hidden skis that appeared from each sill with a rocket booster in the tail providing suitable momentum! Another feature was a self-destruct button, but thankfully glassfibre-bodied replicas, including the wheels, were used for the more explosive scenes, along with two secondhand V8 Saloons. These glassfibre bodies, which were built in Italy, look just like the real thing unless examined closely and AML Ltd sensibly has ensured against misuse of the moulds by

insisting that they remain company property. Apparently, so many screens, windows and bumpers (then £400 apiece) were used during filming that for a while there was a shortage of these items.

To begin with, in *The Living Daylights*, 007 uses Victor Gauntlett's V8 Volante, but this is later shown being 'winterized', to quote Q, in the experimental department with a couple more boffins lowering a saloon roof onto the convertible, the Volante then emerging as the Vantage with all the special equipment. The good news both for Aston fans and the factory is that AML has forged a good relationship with the film company, Eon Productions, and director Cubby Broccoli bought a new V8 Volante for use in California during the making of the film. It thus seems likely that a suitably modified Virage will be James Bond's next Aston Martin mount.

CHAPTER 12

Virage

Launch success marks the way forward

It was not surprising that the world awaited the Virage's debut at the 1988 Birmingham Motor Show with great anticipation – after all, there are not many manufacturers who wait 20 years to introduce a new model, let alone get away with not doing so for such a time. Indeed, once its impending launch was announced, no less than 54 buyers parted with large deposits for an unseen car. Of course, there had been the usual 'scoop' shots of the car undergoing tests, but at that stage not even the name had been chosen. And although a competition was held both at the factory and within the Aston Martin Owners Club for a suitable title – Victor Gauntlett being keen for the new flagship to have a name rather than a letter or number, preferably beginning with V for continuity with Vantage and Volante – it was the Aston chairman himself who came up with the Virage appellation.

A remarkable fact about the Virage is that total development took just two years to complete, despite the fact that it was a brand new model sharing little common componentry with the V8 model it superseded. Thankfully, the Virage also shares little in common with the various press predictions for a new Aston model that had been made during the previous decade, including such 'horrors' as a Mercedes-Cosworth or Jaguar engine. No Aston would be an Aston without its very own engine beating at its heart, an in-house masterpiece recalling all the great racing heritage of days gone by and, hopefully, of those yet to come. Surprisingly, virtually all development mileage was conducted in Britain, the prototype (dark blue to attract as little attention as possible) covering over 70,000 miles with a

second prototype clocking another 40,000 miles.

From the onset in September 1986, it had been decided that the new Aston, designated DP 2034, would continue the tradition of front engine/rear-wheel drive, with all the creature comforts and performance that customers had come to expect. Where it had to differ from the V8 was in its weight and aerodynamic package, with the proviso that the Aston engine powering it must be compatible with lead-free fuel and able to meet the emission laws of both the USA and Europe in 1992 and beyond without any loss in performance. To this end it was clear that four valves per cylinder was the obvious route along which to develop the trusty 5.3-litre V8 engine, and after investigation into costings and the development time required at home in Britain, the engine contract was awarded to Callaway Engineering in Connecticut, USA.

While it is a shame that this work could not have been undertaken by a British firm, such as Cosworth Engineering for example, Reeves Callaway's operation had an excellent pedigree in such matters with considerable four-valve racing experience. It was thus a logical progression that once the four-valve conversion was complete, Callaway should continue developing the V8 – albeit under Aston team manager Richard Williams' guidance – into the lusty race unit that would power the AMR1s and AMR2s. A Vantage version of the Virage, incidentally, was due to become available in late 1990/early 1991, possibly with either supercharging or turbocharging employed. Either way, it was expected to produce around 500bhp and be capable of at

A half-scale model of the new Virage. Behind it, a craftsman works on a prototype chassis.

The Virage's huge 13in ventilated front disc brakes had to be sourced from Australia.

The prototype Virage undergoing tests at the MIRA wind-tunnel.

Twin catalytic converters, sited either side of the transmission, allow the Virage to meet emissions regulations worldwide. It means the USA can at last share proper European Aston performance.

The V8's de Dion/Watts linkage rear suspension has been reworked in aluminium for the Virage, reducing cornering loads into the body while a single mounting reduces road noise.

least 200mph. First, however, the Virage Volante was to become available with a planned launch at the 1990 Birmingham Motor Show.

Callaway Engineering started work on the four-valve conversion of the production Aston V8 in April 1986, completing the work by December 1987. By the time Aston Martin had finalized its installed specification, power for the Weber fuel-injected V8 was quoted at 310bhp with 340lb/ft of torque (against the 305bhp/340lb/ft of the Series 5 V8), quite an achievement considering this was a catalyst-equipped engine, and sufficient to propel the Virage to 60mph in 5 to 6 seconds and on to a 160mph maximum – though, interestingly, 6,000rpm in fifth gear equates to 188mph.

'The goal for the production engine', explains Reeves Callaway, 'was to design, execute and prove the initial durability of the four-valve configuration, and there, essentially, our responsibility ended. Aston's responsibility then started with finalizing for production all the ancilliaries and, most importantly, all the engine management system to comply with the required standards.

'The task was to give Aston the basis for development for the next 10 years; we were not trying to do 10 years' development in one year. With the contract's time and money we were able to give them something conservative and very modern. There was very straightforward thinking on the four valves. Our little company gets involved in all types of four-valves, but this was a design about a known and tested engine – like incorporating a hydraulic chain tensioning system, hydraulic bucket lifters, using a known camshaft profile and using a modern combustion chamber shape that we know. Four valves, of course, go up and down very much more easily than two valves because of their size and the lower friction rates, and the flame power travels far better from a centrally mounted spark plug. And one of the goals was to continue, if not enliven, Aston's image under the hood.'

The Virage's chassis had originally been destined to be all new, but in tune with a desire to rationalize production componentry (and thus increase production from five to six cars per week through simpler assembly), the final chassis design incorporated much of the existing Lagonda, including

The Virage's four-valve V8 in the engine shop at Newport Pagnell.

The 5,340cc Aston V8's new four-valve head casting was developed by Reeves Callaway in the USA.

front bulkhead, chassis rails and crossmember, which were attached to a new platform and rear structure – which is why Aston was able to first test the new four-valve engine in what appeared to be a short-wheelbase, Virage-size Lagonda.

As part of the weight-trimming exercise, the de Dion rear suspension had been earmarked for attention and the new rear chassis section allowed a reworked, lightweight system to

The prototype Virage chassis on the jig.

As always, the Virage's aluminium body panels are hand-rolled and finished by skilled craftsmen. Here one of the prototype's rear wings takes shape.

be adopted using aluminium radius-arms, the triangular redesign of which prevents cornering loads being fed directly into the body, as they had been on previous models. The system's single main mounting also means that less road/tyre noise will be transmitted to the Virage's occupants. At the same time, the rear discs were moved outboard, away from the heat generated by the limited-slip differential, though problems in this area have generally been limited to competition applications with the V8 model. The brake discs are the largest yet seen on an Aston, so much so that the Lockheed 13in ventilated fronts and 11.3in solid rears had to be sourced from Australia, no European manufacturer being able to supply these sizes. The alloy wheels (the design of which came in for criticism at the NEC launch) are also new, though a familiar 8in x 16in size – the Virage Vantage was expected to use 17in diameter rims – clothed in specially developed 255/60 VR16 Avon Turbospeed tyres.

At the front end there had initially been talk of employing Jaguar's twin-wishbone set-up and ironically, in the light of Dearborn's subsequent takeover at Coventry, this path was

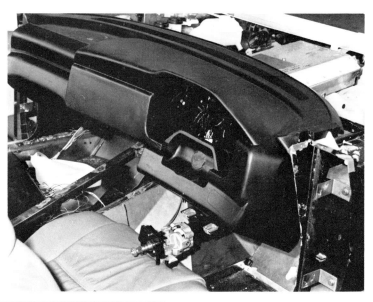

A new-style dashboard for the Virage, but still with analogue instruments, under assembly.

The first Virage chassis being wheeled across Tickford Street, which splits the AML factory, for assembly on the other side. The Virage's platform chassis benefited from CAD and finite element analysis.

The same chassis with most of its aluminium panels in place.

With all running gear in place. Note the distinctive and neat cam covers of the four-valve V8 compared with the two-valve version.

dropped in deference to majority shareholder Ford in late 1987. Aston's own twin-wishbone system was thus employed and as such it should have far greater integrity through Aston's tendency to over-engineer and use aircraft-specification forgings. For the first time, Bilstein shock absorbers replaced the usual Koni items, while one benefit of the Ford merger was the sudden availability of the Sierra Cosworth rack-and-pinion steering which, with suitable modification, proved ideal for the Virage's geometry. It is also higher-geared than the old V8's and uses less power-assistance.

Visually, the Virage shape is a far cry from the V8's, although it cleverly exudes the same aggressive and purposeful aura that promises to deliver the goods, while also retaining the traditionally shaped Aston radiator grille. Five separate British design studios were approached to submit a design for the new Aston, including DBS and Lagonda stylist William Towns, but it was Royal College of Art tutors John Heffernan and Ken Greenley who came up trumps (the pair had previously designed the mid-engined Panther Solo). To some extent they were limited in scope by both the design

The second prototype Virage. The Virage has clean, modern lines from any angle.

A prototype Virage undergoes mandatory crash-testing. Naturally it passed with flying colours.

criteria already laid down by the factory and the short timescale to the car's planned 1988 show debut. This meant risking the transition from a quarter-scale to a full-scale wooden model in one hit, which gave little room for changes, while the interior was produced without the usual luxury of sectionalized drawings.

Fortunately, the gambles paid off, and after extensive wind-tunnel testing at Southampton University, the definitive Virage form was created. That tunnel testing, however, did lead to a redesign of the car's rear, the shape losing some of its smoothness through the need to raise the tail to eliminate rear-end lift. That change also raised the original Cd figure from under 0.30 to 0.35, but the resulting car was one that was pleasing both aerodynamically and to the eye. The Virage's length at 15ft 5in is just an inch longer than the Series 5 V8, as is the width at 6ft 1in, while the weight at 3,947lb is 62lb lighter than the last V8 model, though 147lb heavier than the original DBS V8.

The beautiful body is, as always, in hand-beaten and rolled aluminium, though some 'foreign' parts can be found

The two 1988 Birmingham Motor Show cars before dispatch to the NEC. The black headlamp surrounds were deleted from production models, and the headlamps given a flusher fit. On the extreme right is co-designer John Heffernan. Ken Greenley was the other.

adorning it, such as Audi 100 headlights, VW Scirocco rearlights and Porsche 928 indicators. There is nothing new in such cost-effectiveness, however, the old DBS and DBS V8 models of the late 'sixties, for example, used Ford Cortina Mk2 sidelights and Hillman Hunter rearlight assemblies.

Naturally, the Virage's interior retains all the traditional Aston comforts and luxury, the leather upholstery and wood veneer still being beautifully hand-crafted at Newport Pagnell. The space and design, however, are considerably different from the V8 model's, notably in the width (the wide transmission tunnel still dominates), the roof height and the dashboard layout, the latter retaining white-on-black analogue instrumentation. Compared with the DBS V8/V8

model, headroom is greater, as is rear seat room, though the fully power-adjustable front seats are narrower because of hug-fit side bolstering to better locate the occupants.

Press reaction at the Virage launch was virtually unanimous in its praise, but it was to be early 1990 before any journalists got their hands on a production version due, mainly, to tooling problems and internal difficulties at the factory. Officially, the first Virage was finally delivered on January 5, 1990, though at least one had been quietly delivered to its titled owner during December the previous year. In the meantime, with all UK production, at the maximum rate of six per week, sold out for the first two years, some customers were going to have to be very patient!

CHAPTER 13

Ownership and maintenance

Clubs, specialists and spares

Ownership of any of the Aston Martins and Lagondas covered in this book should be a joy provided that the car is in sound condition and its maintenance schedules have been adhered to. Unfortunately, far too often one hears of someone who has purchased an apparently sound V8 model secondhand only subsequently to discover that it has been 'maintained' by back-street bodgers. However, such occurrences do appear to be becoming more rare as these cars become more collectable and expensive, so attracting the more discerning buyer. On the plus side, the Aston Martin and Lagonda are strong and well-built machines, but there are several troublesome areas that should be inspected before a secondhand purchase is made. Otherwise, extremely costly repairs can ensue, which means that any maladies discovered should be suitably reflected in the purchase price.

There are only two clubs catering for Aston Martin and Lagonda models – the Aston Martin Owners Club and The Lagonda Club (addresses will be found at the end of this chapter). The former, which boasts a worldwide membership of 4,000, caters for all models of both marques bar prewar Lagondas, while The Lagonda Club covers Lagonda models only for its 700 members. Both clubs have technical consultants, who are glad to offer help and advice to members, and my thanks must go to Richard Zethrin, joint AMOC postwar consultant (and until 1990 a longtime director of Aston agent Hyde Vale Garage), for his assistance in compiling the following tips.

Naturally, all the usual visual inspections when buying a secondhand car apply, but with Astons and Lagondas it is those less than obvious weak points which can lead to that extra expense. Beginning with the V8 engine, head gasket failure is quite common, but it is not easily detected; the Aston V8 is not an engine that will easily give the game away by displaying water in the oil or similar symptoms. Indeed, in normal driving, a failed head gasket might never come to light because it is only through hard driving that it becomes really evident. 'The V8s do suffer from head gasket problems', explains Richard Zethrin. 'A lot of people don't realize this. If you drive the car normally, the overflow tank – not the header – on the side of the radiator cowling should be half-full. If it is, take the car out and drive it hard, punish it, using 4,000 to 5,000rpm. The overflow should not have filled up any more, so if you come back and find liquid is pouring out you know the system has pressurized. If you really want to be sure, let the engine cool down, and if the header tank in the 'V' shows signs of emptying, it's blowing out.'

However, there is a further method of determining head gasket failure. 'A normal compression or cylinder leakage test will not show it up', adds Zethrin. 'You've got to get the BMEP (Brake Mean Effective Pressure) up. The only way to check for sure is to get top dead centre, making sure the crankshaft is locked, and build the pressure up to 400 to 500psi using air bottles, but you need special equipment – it's something I designed at Hyde Vale, but not a lot of people have the equipment. If you then get bubbling, the head gasket has gone – it's quite common.'

Oil pressure on the Aston V8 engine can vary enormously and anything between 5 and 20psi at idle when hot is quite normal, while at 3,000rpm the gauge should show between 70 and 80psi. Low oil pressure, however, need not necessarily mean renewing bottom end bearings or worse, particularly on cars produced before early 1980. 'If the engine shows approximately 50psi at 3,000rpm', continues Zethrin, 'and zero at idle, it can be that a crankshaft aluminium core plug has come out. There is one on the end big-end journal and all it means is the core plug has come out and so created a large oil gallery, allowing the pressure to drop. It's quite common for the core plug to drop out – though it could be worse. Also, don't be alarmed if you drive away when the engine's cold and the oil pressure rises to 80 and suddenly flicks back to 65, then as you slow down it rises again, then flicks back. Don't worry – it's an in-built prevention against excess oil pressure.'

The Bosch fuel injection system fitted to DBS V8 and early AM V8 models is much maligned for unreliability, but if properly set up, a fuel-injected car can be a very rewarding and quick machine. For anyone in doubt, and this could include some who service Astons for a living, the real way to calibrate the fuel injection system can be found in an excellent article written by Andy Chapman in the Summer 1984 issue of *AM Magazine*, the quarterly publication of the AMOC. Andy, the club's other postwar technical consultant and proprietor of Aston agent Chapman Spooner, has vast experience of this Bosch system and if one follows his instructions, the result could be a very sweet-running V8.

On the subject of induction, Richard Zethrin adds that early carburettor-equipped cars with an S suffix to their engine numbers, indicating different camshafts, do suffer from noisy valve gear. 'The noise is caused by a combination of factors, but you must go to an Aston expert to diagnose it. The cause could be the camshaft profiles – they don't lend themselves to silent running when worn – and worn valve guides.'

Most Aston Martins bar the V8 Vantage and V8 Vantage Zagato and all Lagonda models are fitted with the Chrysler Torqueflite automatic transmission as standard. Numerous oil leaks are commonplace, one in particular often being caused by the failure of the small oil seal where the main control shaft goes through the gearbox, particularly on high-mileage cars. As with other automatic gearboxes, poor gearchanges can often merely be due to a low oil level. However, a tinkling or cracking noise on tickover and in gear, when changing from forward to reverse, or sometimes when pulling away, can indicate cracked torque converter plates, necessitating a rebuild. Similar action will be needed if the transmission oil is black, or it emits a burnt odour. Manual ZF gearboxes are prone to 'knocking' on tickover, which is often eliminated by depressing the clutch and is usually caused, according to Richard, by an uneven engine idle speed. Clutch slip can similarly be simply cured, the cause often being the actuator rod 'bottoming out' in the clutch hydraulic slave cylinder. Remedying this can also cure a high pedal, when clutch engagement takes place at the top of the pedal's travel, otherwise indicating a possibly worn clutch.

Still with the transmission train, if the limited-slip differential tends to 'chatter' when pulling away from rest while turning (for example, at a T-junction), the noise is usually caused by the clutch plates. This can be cured by using gear oil additive available from Aston Martin agents or normal retail outlets. 'But beware', says Zethrin, 'it can also be the differential assembly breaking up, but not the crownwheel and pinion. Again, get expert advice.'

While replacement parts generally are easily obtainable, the differential fitted to early DBS V8 models, identified by its four-bolt nose fixing, is no longer available from Aston Martin. Originally supplied by GKN, parts may be obtainable from this source, otherwise a later unit will have to be fitted. The latter, incidentally, uses internal parts as found in Jaguar XJ6, XJ12 and XJ-S models, so it might be possible to make a saving here.

Front and rear suspension on all models should be subjected to normal checks and it is worth noting that Lagonda Series 2, 3 and 4 models use some Jaguar-sourced components such as the front uprights. A droning from the rear could indicate either a worn differential or worn hub bearings, while in extreme cases a sloppy rear end could be due to the radius-arms about to part company with the floorpan. At the front, thoroughly check the brake reaction strut rubbers on carburettor cars – replacing these involves removing the front suspension and is a lengthy job. Earlier cars used a different design, easier to replace. Steering racks should be inspected for leaking gaiters and if the pinion seal is weeping it can be replaced in situ. Fluid in the gaiters, however, indicates failed internal seals and will necessitate a rack overhaul. The power steering pumps rarely give trouble.

The shock absorbers – Konis are fitted as standard – commonly fail if a car is little used, regardless of age or mileage, says Zethrin. 'The shocks are very prone to seizing if the car is left standing, stored for a long time, or jacked up for long periods.'

Any corrosion of the alloy wheels fitted to Aston and Lagonda Series 1 models – the Series 2 Lagonda uses Jaguar steel items and the Series 3 and 4 BBS rims – is easily spotted, but note that there are two types of alloy wheel. Early cars up to 1976 used a tubed-tyre type and this is now virtually obsolete, so if corrosion is really bad one must consider replacement with the later wheel. This tubeless type is identified by a smooth-edged rim and a smoother profile to the inner casting, and it bolts straight on. As an alternative to the latter, the much later BBS alloy wheels (different from those on the Series 3 and 4 Lagonda) can be fitted, but this would also require an expensive hub change.

Behind those wheels, of course, are the all-important brakes. Juddering through the steering wheel at moderate speeds and vibration of the gearlever in automatic-transmission cars usually indicates brake disc problems. 'The vibration, 99% of the time, means the front discs need replacing', explains Zethrin, 'although a visual inspection and run-out check may show no problems. This is caused by a material difference in the surface of the disc. It is surprising how good and pleasant the brakes normally are to use, but how horrible they are when they're wrong.'

At the rear, the inboard discs on all models (bar the Virage, which has outboard units) can suffer from the ingress of water. 'The rear discs are very prone to corrosion, being three-part – the disc hub, the disc and the retaining ring. One gets a build-up of corrosion between these components which splits the retaining ring away. Replacement is necessary and, indeed, advisable if there are any signs of corrosion, and it can be worth having the calipers replaced as well. None of the discs are interchangeable and they do vary from model to model.' Again it should be remembered that the Series 2, 3 and 4 Lagondas employ Jaguar XJ brake discs and calipers front and rear. If everything is found to be in order and the brake pedal appears hard, the cause is usually either a vacuum or a servo problem. 'Vacuum valves are the first things to check. The early ones are aluminium, the later ones plastic; the plastic type give very few problems. The obvious check is that you're not losing vacuum elsewhere.

'Vacuum pipe problems are the most common cause of air conditioning failure on many earlier cars', adds Zethrin, 'usually following the fitment of a radio, when the centre console is disturbed by someone unaware of what lies beneath. It's very rare to find it working correctly; it was never the best system in the world, despite many changes. On early cars to 1983 a multitude of vacuum pipes are hidden under the centre console and they can be fitted incorrectly or not at all. This can also lead to a hard brake pedal and a loss of vacuum.'

Electrical problems on Aston variants and Series 1 Lagondas are minimal, one of the biggest failures being rear lamps. Usually this is due to a fault with the bulb holder, which can be bought separately rather than as a part of the whole unit. The high-tech system fitted to later model Lagondas, however, can cause more than a few headaches, particularly early Series 2 cars. Indeed, a degree in auto electronics would be an asset here! 'Electrical problems can be numerous', continues Zethrin, 'and the air conditioning is extremely complex and very troublesome. The touch panels in the doors corrode, affecting the central locking. The electrics are too complicated for their own good; there are relays everywhere.'

One of the most critical areas to inspect when buying a secondhand Aston Martin or Lagonda must be the chassis, particularly on the older models, where corrosion can be a major and costly problem. 'Beware of anybody saying it only needs the sills done', warns Zethrin, 'it's very rare that it's just the sills. It can be the sills, the outriggers, inner chassis sections, front door sections, engine bay and front inner wheelarches, rear radius-arm area, spare wheel well, the doors, front and rear screen apertures, the bottom of front and rear wings and the rear chassis sections under the boot floor. Special attention should be given to this as proper repairs can be very expensive. If one does undertake this sort of work, make sure the job is done properly – there is too much plating over. All rot, all corrosion, must be cut out and new panels fabricated. Enormous care should be taken and a specialist inspection is imperative.' Lagonda Series 2, 3 and 4 models are less prone to the corrosion that attacks the DBS V8 and V8 types, but watch out for corrosion around the door shuts, where water becomes trapped under the rubber, also the rear door apertures.

The pitfalls of chassis work can be many and it is just as easy for someone to bodge an Aston Martin or Lagonda as any other marque. As an example, Zethrin cites the case of a Hyde Vale customer who was quoted about £8,000 for remedial chassis work. Unprepared to pay this figure, the customer went elsewhere and some months later brought the Aston back to Hyde Vale for a routine service, boasting how the chassis work had been completed at a cost of just £2,000. He was less impressed and somewhat ashen-faced when it was pointed out that beneath the fresh underseal lay pieces of old oil cans pop-riveted in place!

As an indication of the sort of work that can be involved, corrosion around the screen apertures can appear minor. However, this is caused by the screen trim clips collecting water and it comes from inside the aperture. Curing this properly requires removal of the screen, drilling out the clips, shot blasting the affected area and applying an anti-corrosive treatment; an expensive job.

Naturally, all the above comments apply to V8 Volante models, but there are also a couple of areas to watch with the latter. Very early V8 Volantes left the factory without any chassis strengthening, but it was soon discovered that this caused excessive scuttle shake, so soon after production began a subframe was added to the rear floorpan. Most previous models have since been recalled for this fitment, but make sure the subframe, nicknamed the 'garden gate', is in place, bolted to the rear passenger floor and spare wheel well. It does have the disadvantage of reducing clearance for the exhaust system, and occasional banging of the exhaust pipe as a consequence is not unusual.

Hood catches and their correct operation for the convertible top are another point to check. 'The early hood catches have no safety catch', explains Zethrin, 'the slightly later type have a sliding safety catch, and the later type similar but beefier catches. The very latest type also have a central locking device adjacent to the mirror.

'The hood is also prone to ripping adjacent to where it meets the rear of the glass in the area of the Velcro; it rips where it rises from the Velcro to follow the back window. Above the rear window there is a wooden frame and this can be prone to rotting; the cant rail can also rot. One might find that one needs a frame and a cant rail as well as a hood, so a new hood can be expensive. Later cars have a glass rear window, which is much neater and tidier.

'The Volantes also rust at the top of the windscreen and corrosion can develop in the cant rail gulley. Also watch out for body cracks radiating from the fuel filler apertures, caused by metal fatigue. The hood hydraulic motors don't give many problems, but it must be noted that you have to help the hood on its initial movement; a helping hand is necessary.'

The above comments are intended as a useful guideline to anyone considering the purchase of a secondhand Aston Martin or Lagonda and to highlight the need to take expert advice. These cars are not cheap to buy or maintain and, having settled on a price – one that hopefully takes into consideration any work that might be required – it is worth working out annual running and insurance costs. As the auction market has shown, Aston Martins in particular have become a target for the speculators, which has pushed prices artificially high. By the beginning of 1990, prices had resumed a more realistic level, but whichever way one looks at it, these cars are undoubted investments. However, don't despair – just be wary and enjoy. Also, as Richard Zethrin concludes: 'Don't necessarily be put off by a high-mileage car which has been used regularly. Very often, some low-mileage cars prove to be not so good. For a well-maintained V8 Aston, 100,000 miles is nothing.'

Some proprietary parts from other manufacturers' products are fitted to Aston Martin and Lagonda V8 models. Listed below are some of them, which may help to keep down maintenance and repair costs!

Air cleaner, DBS V8 flat type – Jaguar XJ6.
Starter motor, all V8 models – Chrysler.

Front side/indicator lights, DBS V8 – Ford Cortina Mk2.
Front side/indicator lights, all AM V8 models to date – MG MGB.
Rear light assembly, DBS V8 and early AM V8 – Hillman Hunter.
Indicator stalk, later models – Vauxhall Astra/Opel Kadett.
Electric switches – Mercedes-Benz and others (Bosch).
Front brake caliper, all Aston models – Lamborghini Miura.

Club addresses:
Aston Martin Owners Club
1A High Street
Sutton
Nr ELY
Cambridgeshire CB6 2RB

The Lagonda Club
68 Savill Road
Lindfield
HAYWARDS HEATH
Sussex RH16 2NN

Two Series 1 V8 Vantages and a Series 2 model line up on the grid at an AMOC Horsfall meeting at Silverstone.

APPENDIX A

Aston Martin and Lagonda introduction dates (UK)

Aston Martin DBS V8	September 1969	Aston Martin AM V8 Vantage Series 3	October 1986
Aston Martin AM V8 Series 2	May 1972	Aston Martin AM V8 Vantage Volante	October 1986
Aston Martin AM V8 Series 3	August 1973	Aston Martin AM V8 Volante Zagato	March 1987
Aston Martin AM V8 Vantage	February 1977	Aston Martin V8 Lagonda	October 1974
Aston Martin AM V8 Volante	June 1978	Aston Martin Lagonda Series 2	October 1976
Aston Martin AM V8 Series 4	October 1978	Aston Martin Lagonda Series 3	January 1986
Aston Martin AM V8 Vantage Series 2	October 1978	Aston Martin Lagonda Series 4	March 1987
Aston Martin AM V8 Series 5	January 1986	Aston Martin Virage	October 1988
Aston Martin AM V8 Volante Series 2	January 1986	Aston Martin Virage Volante	September 1990
Aston Martin AM V8 Vantage Zagato	March 1986		

APPENDIX B

V8 Aston Martin specifications

DBS V8 (1969 to 1972)

Engine: V8-cylinder, all-alloy, twin overhead camshafts per bank, 64° included angle, 85 x 100mm, 5,340cc, CR 9.0:1, Bosch fuel injection, 320bhp @ 5,000rpm.

Transmission: ZF all-synchromesh 5-speed manual or Chrysler Torqueflite 3-speed automatic (no price differential). Axle ratio 3.54:1 manual, 3.33:1 automatic. Overall gear ratios, manual: 2.99, 3.54, 4.32, 6.30, 10.27, reverse 9.31:1; overall gear ratios, automatic: 3.33, 4.83, 8.16, reverse 7.33:1; 26.6mph/1,000rpm in manual top gear, 23.9mph/1,000rpm in automatic top gear. Limited-slip differential standard on all models.

Suspension: Front, unequal-length wishbones/coil springs, co-axial dampers, anti-roll bar; rear, de Dion axle, radius arms, Watts linkage, coil springs. Armstrong Selectaride dampers.

Steering: Adwest power-assisted rack and pinion.

Brakes: Girling ventilated discs, 10.75 x 1.25in outboard front, 10.38 x 1.25in inboard rear, vacuum servo-assisted.

Wheels: Aston Martin alloy 15 x 7in; tyres Pirelli Cinturato GR70 VR15.

Chassis: Rigid steel platform with aluminium 2-door coupe coachwork, dual 5½in quartz-iodine headlamps, full-width front grille.

Dimensions: Wheelbase 8ft 6¾in, front track 4ft 11in, rear track 4ft 11in, length 15ft 0½in, width 6ft 0in, height 4ft 4¼in. Fuel tank 21gal. Unladen weight 3,800lb. **Price:** £6,897.

AM V8 S2 (1972 to 1973)

As DBS V8 except Lucas Opus transistorized ignition, dual 7in quartz-iodine headlamps, shorter recessed front grille, spare wheel laid flat in boot rather than upright. 3.33:1 axle ratio standardized for manual-transmission cars, 2.88:1 for automatic-transmission cars. Overall gear ratios, manual: 2.83, 3.33, 4.06, 5.93, 9.66, reverse 8.78:1; overall gear ratios, automatic: 2.88, 4.20, 7.05, reverse 6.34:1; 27.8mph/1,000rpm in manual top gear, 27.3mph/1,000rpm in automatic top gear. Length 15ft 3in. **Price:** £8,949.

AM V8 S3 (1973 to 1978)

As AM V8 S2 except fuel injection replaced by 4 Weber 42 DCNF carburettors, larger bonnet bulge. Power 320bhp @ 5,000rpm, from June 1977 304bhp @ 5,500rpm. Improved engine and transmission cooling, ventilation louvres below rear window deleted in favour of lip. Revised switchgear, larger ashtray, improved seats, central locking for passenger door, increased heat and sound insulation. Armstrong Selectaride dampers dropped in favour of conventional units. Options of 3.07:1 axle ratio with automatic transmission and 3.54:1 with manual transmission. Overall gear ratios with automatic 3.07:1 option: 3.07, 4.45, 7.52, reverse 6.75:1; 26.4mph/1,000rpm in top gear. Pirelli tyres replaced by Avons. From 1975 manual transmission £355 optional extra. Length 15ft 3¾in. **Price:** £9,593.

AM V8 S4 (1978 to 1986)

As AM V8 S3 except with built-in rear boot spoiler, redesigned bonnet without air intake, revised damper settings, stainless steel exhaust system. Wood veneer for dashboard and door trim as first introduced on V8 Volante, leather rather than cloth roof lining, restyled seat headrests, new centre console with rear passenger cigarette lighter, improved air conditioning. After June 1980 engine fitted with larger, tuftrided valves, different camshaft profiles, cylinder head porting standardized with V8 Vantage, barrel-shaped pistons, CR raised to 9.3:1, carburettor and distributors revised. Power still quoted as 304bhp @ 5,500rpm but with improved fuel economy. USA engines, CR reduced from 8.5 to 8.0:1. Engine number coding changed from V/540 to V/580. Automatic lock-up for automatic transmission with cruise control option. Central locking for both doors, gas struts for bonnet, interior switches for petrol filler cap and boot lock, lamp failure warning light, electrically adjusted door mirrors. After 1983 8in wide BBS alloy wheels became standard equipment, air conditioning uprated again. Manual transmission £1,000 option but after 1979 available once more at no extra cost until reintroduced as £1,280 option in June 1985. **Price:** £23,000.

AM V8 S5 (1986 to 1989)

As AM V8 S4 except Weber/Marelli instead of Bosch fuel injection, power now 305bhp @ 5,000rpm with 320lb/ft torque. Flat bonnet without scoop. Engine number coding changed from V/580 to V/585. BBS wheels introduced on late V8 S4 still standard equipment. 3.058:1 axle ratio standard on cars with automatic transmission. Overall gear ratios, automatic: 3.058, 4.43, 7.49, reverse 6.73:1; 27.0mph/1,000rpm in automatic top gear. Manual transmission again a no extra cost option. Length 15ft 4in, weight 4,009lb. **Price:** £55,000.

AM V8 Vantage (1977 to 1978)

As AM V8 S3 except power output 380bhp @ 6,000rpm with approx 380lb/ft torque @ 4,000rpm (no official figures released), via larger inlet valves, revised camshafts, CR 9.5:1, quadruple Weber 48 IDA carburettors, modified inlet manifold and airbox. ZF 5-speed transmission standard with (officially) no automatic option. Stiffer suspension and Koni dampers, 250/60 VR15 Pirelli CN12 tyres. Separate boot spoiler, deeper front air dam, blanked-off radiator grille and bonnet scoop, Perspex headlamp covers. **Price:** £20,000.

AM V8 Vantage S2 (1978 to 1986)

As AM V8 Vantage except CR 9.3:1, boot spoiler now integral part of coachwork as on AM V8 S4. **Price:** £26,000.

AM V8 Vantage S3 (1986 to 1989)

As AM V8 Vantage S2 except power now 400bhp via higher-lift camshafts, larger ports and CR 10.2:1. Option of 432bhp as fitted to V8 Vantage Zagato using Weber 50 IDA carburettors, twin plenum chamber and larger-bore exhaust system. BBS 16 x 8in wheels; Goodyear Eagle 255/50 VR16 tyres. **Price:** £63,500.

AM V8 Vantage Zagato (1986 to 1990)

Engine: As AM V8 Vantage S3 except Weber 48 IDA carburettors bored out to 50mm, new twin plenum chamber and larger-bore exhaust system, 432bhp @ 6,000rpm, torque 395lb/ft @ 5,100rpm. Transmission, brakes and suspension as AM V8 Vantage S3 but with 3.062:1 axle ratio. Overall gear ratios 2.60, 3.06, 3.73, 5.45, 8.88, reverse 8.05:1; 25.0mph/1,000rpm in top gear. Unique Speedline 16 x 8in alloy wheels and 255/50 Goodyear Eagle tyres. Chassis as AM V8 S5 and AM V8 Vantage S3 but with shorter, lighter 2-door body by Zagato of Milan with flush-fitting glass, bootlid spoiler, front spoiler, deformable GRP bumpers, traditional Aston Martin grille shape and Zagato 'double blister' trademark on roof. Dimensions: Wheelbase 8ft 6¾in, front track 4ft 11in, rear track 4ft 11in, length 14ft 4¾in, width 6ft 1¾in, height 4ft 3in. Fuel tank 21gal. Unladen weight 3,637lb. **Price:** £87,000.

AM V8 Volante Zagato (1987 to 1990)

As AM V8 Vantage Zagato except fuel-injected 305bhp engine as AM V8 S5, no bonnet bulge, fractionally longer convertible coachwork, modified front grille with headlamp 'eyelid' covers. Dimensions as AM V8 Vantage Zagato except length 14ft 8½in, height 4ft 3¼in. Unladen weight 3,714lb. **Price: £125,000.**

AM V8 Volante (1978 to 1986)

As AM V8 S4 except with convertible coachwork, no bootlid spoiler, power-operated hood, sensor connected to handbrake to prevent hood operation at standstill. Wood veneer introduced for dashboard and door trim, bonnet air intake blanked-off as AM V8 Vantage. Officially not available in Vantage specification. After June 1980 same modifications as to AM V8 S4. Dimensions as AM V8 S4 except height 4ft 6in. Unladen weight 3,950lb. **Price:** £33,864.

AM V8 Volante S2 (1986 to 1989)

As AM V8 Volante except fuel-injected 305bhp engine specification and other improvements as AM V8 S5 but without integral bootlid spoiler. Additional hood central safety catch. Unladen weight 4,009lb. **Price:** £68,500.

AM V8 Vantage Volante (1986 to 1989)

As AM V8 Volante except AM V8 Vantage S3 400bhp engine (and 432bhp option) and mechanical specification, deeper front air dam and rear valance, integral bootlid spoiler, wider (than V8 Vantage S3) wheelarches integrated with sill skirts. 16 x 8in BBS alloy wheels, 255/50-16 Goodyear Eagle tyres. **Price:** £93,500.

AM Virage (From 1989)

Engine: V8-cylinder, all-alloy, 4 valves per cylinder, twin overhead camshafts per bank, 64° included angle, 85 x 100mm, 5,340cc, CR 9.5:1, Weber fuel injection, 310bhp @ 6,000rpm, torque 340lb/ft @ 3,700rpm, unleaded fuel, catalyst-equipped.

Transmission: ZF all-synchromesh 5-speed manual or Chrysler Torqueflite 3-speed automatic (no price differential). Axle ratio 3.062:1 manual or automatic. Overall gear ratios, manual: 2.587, 3.062, 3.736, 5.540, 8.874, reverse 8.053:1; overall gear ratios, automatic: 3.062, 4.440, 7.502, reverse 6.736:1; 31.3mph/1,000rpm in manual top gear, 26.5mph/1,000rpm in automatic top gear. Limited-slip differential standard on all models.

Suspension: Front, unequal-length wishbones/coil springs, co-axial spring dampers, anti-roll bar; rear, aluminium de Dion axle, aluminium triangulated radius-arms, Watts linkage, dual-rate coil springs, telescopic dampers.

Steering: Adwest power-assisted rack and pinion.

Brakes: Lockheed ventilated discs, 13.0 x 1.11in outboard front, 11.3 x 0.61in outboard rear, AP aluminium calipers, vacuum servo-assisted.

Wheels: Aston Martin aluminium alloy 16 x 8in; tyres Avon 255/60 VR16.

Chassis: Rigid steel platform with aluminium 2-door coupe bodywork, flush-fitting glass, rectangular headlamps, bootlip spoiler, front spoiler, deformable GRP bumpers, traditional Aston Martin grille shape.

Dimensions: Wheelbase 8ft 6¾in, front track 4ft 11½in, rear track 5ft 0in, length 15ft 6½in, width 6ft 1in, height 4ft 4in. Fuel tank 24.8gal. Unladen weight 3,946lb. **Price:** £120,000.

AM Virage Volante (From 1990)

As AM Virage except convertible coachwork. No further details available prior to anticipated September 1990 launch at NEC Birmingham Motor Show.

APPENDIX C

V8 Lagonda specifications

AM V8 Lagonda (1974 to 1976)

As AM V8 except 4-door lengthened coachwork, metallic paintwork and restyled Lagonda grille. Headlamp wash/wipe, central locking on all doors, interior switches for petrol filler cap and boot lock, stereo/casette with recording facility. Dimensions as AM V8 except length 16ft 2in, height 4ft 5¼in. Unladen weight 4,400lb. **Price:** £14,040.

AM V8 Lagonda S2 (1976 to 1986)

Engine: As AM V8 S3 except 280bhp @ 5,000rpm.
Transmission: Chrysler Torqueflite 3-speed automatic, no manual option. Axle ratio 3.07:1. Overall gear ratios 3.07, 4.45, 7.52, reverse 6.75:1. 26.4mph/1,000rpm in top gear. Limited-slip differential standard.
Suspension: As AM V8 S3 layout except self-levelling rear dampers.
Steering and brakes: As AM V8 S3.
Wheels: Steel 15 x 7in with stainless steel brake-cooling hubcaps.
Chassis: Rigid steel platform with sleek all-new aluminium 4-door saloon coachwork, 4 pop-up headlamps, waistline rubbing strip. Digital, cathode ray instrumentation with push-button electronic switchgear – electronic gearchange deleted late 1978. After October 1983 BBS 15 x 7in alloy wheels, USA-specification bumpers and spoilers standardized. Bespoiled Tickford version with 2 colour televisions also available at £85,000. After October 1984 dashboard featured multilingual verbal accompaniment. Limited-edition long-wheelbase version available at £110,000.
Dimensions: Wheelbase 9ft 6½in, front track 5ft 0½in, rear track 5ft 1½in, length 17ft 4in, width 5ft 11½in, height 4ft 3¼in. Fuel tank 23gal. Unladen weight 3,800lb, after 1982 4,551lb. **Price:** £24,570.

AM V8 Lagonda S3 (1986 to 1987)

As AM V8 Lagonda S2 except Weber/Marelli fuel injection as AM V8 S5, 300bhp (240bhp USA) @ 5,000rpm. After 1987 vacuum fluorescent instrumentation and 3.058:1 axle ratio. Overall gear ratios 3.058, 4.43, 7.49, reverse 6.73:1; 25.8mph/1,000rpm in top gear. Unladen weight 4,662lb. **Price:** £79,500.

AM V8 Lagonda S4 (1987 to 1990)

As AM V8 Lagonda S3 except same specification 305bhp engine as AM V8 S5, 16 x 7in alloy wheels and 255/60 VR15 Avon CR27 tyres. Coachwork 'rounded off' using all new panels, deep front spoiler with foglamps, sill skirts, fuel fillers relocated from C-pillar to below rear screen, rubbing strips deleted, pop-up headlamps replaced by 6 external units, electronic touch buttons replaced by push-buttons. Axle ratio 3.07:1 as AM V8 Lagonda S2. Unladen weight 4,547lb. **Price:** £95,000.

APPENDIX D

V8 chassis numbers and production runs

DBS V8	DBSV8/10001/R – DBSV8/10405/RCA
AM V8 S2	V8/10501/RCA – V8/10789/RCA
AM V8 S3	V8/11002/RCA – V8/12000/RCA;
	V8/12010/RCA – V8/12031/RCA
AM V8 S4	V8SOR 12032 – V8SOR 12499
AM V8 S5	V8SGR 12500 – V8VKR 12701
AM V8 Volante	V8COR 15001 – V8CFR 15439 (*15292
	not used)
AM V8 Volante S2	V8CGL 15400 – V8CKR 15849
AM V8 Vantage Z	V8XGR 20010 – V8ZJR 20062 (*except
	20042)
AM V8 Volante Z	V8XGR 20042 & V8ZJR 30010 – V8ZKR
	30043
AM Virage	AMIS9LBR 50000 – production continues
AM V8 Lagonda	L/12001/RCAC – L/12007/RCAC
AM V8 Lagonda S2	L/13001/R – LOFR 13463
AM V8 Lagonda S3	LOFR 13464 – LOHR 13539
AM V8 Lagonda S4	LOHR 13540 – LOJR 13645

Note 1: V8 Vantage models identified by suffix V up to September 1978, thereafter by prefix V after V8 in chassis number, ie: first V8 Vantage chassis number is V8/11563/RCA<u>V</u> while first V8 Vantage S2 number is V8<u>V</u>OR 12040. V8 Vantage S3 models with 432bhp option have X prefix in place of V, the same coding applying to V8 Vantage Volante models. Unlike V8 Volante models, which effectively use a different chassis, V8 Vantages do not have their own run of chassis numbers; all V8 Volante chassis numbers begin 15.......

Note 2: Circa 1983 a lengthy and complicated new chassis numbering system was introduced for USA-bound cars with specific dating designed to foil the unscrupulous actions of some traders. This new coding, beginning SCFC..... was soon adopted for all models regardless of destination, but to simplify matters only the relevant lettering/numbering under the old system is reproduced here. For example, the last V8 Saloon produced was a Vantage model with the chassis number SCFC<u>V81V5</u>K<u>TR</u> 12701 – the letters and numbers underlined correspond to the old chassis coding, thus V8 refers to the model type, V to Vantage, K is consecutive to J (Series 5 having commenced with G) and R signifies right-hand drive.

APPENDIX E

V8 production engine identification numbers

DBS V8	V/540/....
AM V8 S2	V/540/....
AM V8 S3	V/540/....
AM V8 S4	V/540/.... until June 1980, thereafter
	V/580/....
AM V8 S5	V/585/....
AM V8 Vantage	V/540/....V
AM V8 Vantage S2	V/540/....V until June 1980, thereafter
	V/580/....V
AM V8 Vantage S3	V/580/..../V or X
AM V8 Volante	V/540/.... until June 1980, thereafter
	V/580/....
AM V8 Volante S2	V/585/....
AM V8 Vantage Z	V/580/....
AM V8 Volante Z	V/540/....
AM V8 Virage	89/5..../
AM V8 Lagonda	V/540/....
AM V8 Lagonda S2	V/540/.... until June 1980, thereafter
	V/580/....
AM V8 Lagonda S3	V/585/....
AM V8 Lagonda S4	V/585/....

Note: EE suffix to engine number indicates USA emission specification; CAC indicates Coolair air conditioning, automatic transmission and cosmic fire metallic paintwork; A or M suffix to Virage engine numbers indicates automatic or manual transmission.

APPENDIX F

V8 Aston Martin and Lagonda performance figures

	DBS V8	AM V8 S3	AM V8 S4(A)	AM V8 Vtg	AM V8 Vtg S2	AM V8 Vol(A)	AM V8 Lag
Max speed (mph)	160	155	146	170(E)	168(E)	140(E)	145
Acceleration (sec)							
0–30mph	2.6	2.3	2.8	2.2	2.3	3.7	3.2
0–40mph	3.3	3.2	3.9	2.8	3.0	4.8	4.7
0–50mph	4.5	4.6	5.1	3.8	4.3	6.1	6.2
0–60mph	5.9	5.7	6.6	5.4	5.2	7.7	7.9
0–70mph	7.4	7.2	8.3	6.9	6.5	9.6	10.3
0–80mph	9.1	8.9	10.6	8.5	8.1	11.7	12.8
0–90mph	11.5	11.2	13.1	10.8	9.9	14.1	16.0
0–100mph	13.8	13.6	16.0	13.0	11.9	17.3	20.2
0–110mph	17.0	16.8	20.1	15.8	14.5	21.9	25.3
0–120mph	21.8	20.5	25.2	20.7	18.2	28.0	32.9
Standing ¼-mile	14.3	14.1	14.8	13.7	13.4	15.6	16.1
Direct top gear*							
20–40mph	5.6	–	2.3(1)	8.5	–	2.4(1)	
30–50mph	5.4	7.0	2.4(1)	7.2	–	2.4(1)	2.9
40–60mph	5.3	6.9	2.6(1)	6.9	7.7	3.1(1)	2.9
50–70mph	5.0	6.7	3.6(2)	6.8	6.3	3.8(2)	3.3
60–80mph	5.0	6.2	4.1(2)	6.8	5.9	4.1(2)	4.2
70–90mph	5.1	6.4	6.1	7.1	6.2	4.7(2)	4.9
80–100mph	5.4	6.8	5.9	7.4	6.4	6.4	6.5
90–110mph	6.0	7.5	7.2	7.9	6.9	8.5	8.4
100–120mph	–	8.7	9.0	8.9	7.5	11.2	9.7
Overall cons (mpg)	12.9	13.2	13.3	13.5	11.3	13.6	12.5
Unladen wgt (lb)	3800	3886	3969	4001	3931	3954	11.8
Test date	1971	1973	1982	1977	1981	1979	–
Source	Motor	Motor	Autocar	Autocar	Motor	Motor	1980 Motor

* Except for automatic gearbox where highest gear is indicated in brackets.   (E) means estimated speed.

Factory performance figures

	AM V8 S5	AM V8 Vol S2	AM V8 Vtg Zag	AM V8 Vtg Vol	AM V8 Lag S4
Max speed (mph)	150	150	186	164	143
0–60mph	6.7	6.7	4.8	5.4	8.9